RENEWING ✠ WORSHIP

Principles
for Worship

Evangelical Lutheran Church in America
Published by Augsburg Fortress

RENEWING WORSHIP 2
Principles for Worship

This resource has been prepared by the Evangelical Lutheran Church in America for provisional use.

Scripture quotations, unless otherwise noted, are from the New Revised Standard Version Bible © 1989 Division of Christian Education of the National Council of Churches of Christ in the United States of America. Used by permission.

Prayers and liturgical texts acknowledged as *LBW* are copyright © 1978 *Lutheran Book of Worship* and those acknowledged as *With One Voice* are copyright © 1995 Augsburg Fortress.

The Use of the Means of Grace: A Statement on the Practice of Word and Sacrament, included as the appendix in this volume, was adopted for guidance and practice by the Fifth Biennial Churchwide Assembly of the Evangelical Lutheran Church in America, August 19, 1997. Copyright © 1997 Evangelical Lutheran Church in America, administered by Augsburg Fortress. Available separately, ISBN 0-8066-3648-3.

ACKNOWLEDGMENTS
Design and production: Eric Vollen, design; Jessica Hillstrom, editorial production; Carolyn Porter of The Kantor Group, Inc., book design; Nicholas Markell, logo design

The paper used in this publication meets the minimum requirements of American National Standard for Information Sciences—Permanence of Paper for Printed Library Materials, ANSI Z329.48-1984.

Manufactured in the U.S.A. ISBN 0-8066-7003-7

06 05 04 03 02   1   2   3   4   5

Contents

Preface

In the years since the publication of *Lutheran Book of Worship* in 1978, the pace of change both within the church and beyond has quickened. The past three decades have seen not only a growing ecumenical consensus but also a deepened focus on the church's mission to the world. The church has embraced broadened understandings of culture, increasing musical diversity, changes in the usage of language, a renewed understanding of the central pattern of Christian worship, and an explosion of electronic media and technologies. These shifts have had a profound effect on the weekly assembly gathered around word and sacrament. The present situation calls for a renewal of worship and of common resources for worship, a renewal grounded in the treasures of the church's history while open to the possibilities of the future.

Renewing Worship is a response to these emerging changes in the life of the church and the world. Renewing Worship includes a series of provisional resources intended to provide worship leaders with a range of proposed strategies and materials that address the various liturgical and musical needs of the church. These resources are offered to assist the renewal of corporate worship in a variety of settings, especially among Lutheran churches, in anticipation of the next generation of primary worship resources.

Published on a semiannual basis beginning in 2001, this series includes hymns and songs (newly written or discovered as well as new approaches to common texts and tunes), liturgical texts and music for weekly and seasonal use, occasional rites (such as marriage, healing, and burial), resources for daily prayer (morning prayer, evening prayer, and prayer at the close of the day), psalms and canticles, prayers and lectionary texts, and other supporting materials. Over the course of several years, worship leaders will have the opportunity to obtain and evaluate a wide range of Renewing Worship resources both in traditional print format and in electronic form delivered via the Internet at www.renewingworship.org.

These published resources, however, are only one component of the Renewing Worship multi-year plan led by the Evangelical Lutheran Church in America (ELCA) as it enters the next generation of its worship life. Endorsed by the ELCA Church Council and carried out in partnership by the ELCA Division for Congregational Ministries and the ELCA Publishing House (Augsburg Fortress), this plan for worship renewal includes five components. The first phase (2001-2002), a consultative process to develop principles for language, music, preaching, and worship space, is more fully described in the introduction to *Principles for Worship* that follows.

The second phase (2001-2005) includes a series of editorial teams that collect, develop, and revise worship materials for provisional use. The liturgical and musical resource proposals that emerge from the editorial teams are to be published during the third phase of this plan (also in 2001-2005) as trial-use resources in the Renewing Worship series. These materials include proposals for newly developed, ecumenically shared, or recently revised texts, rites, and music. Crucial to this phase will be careful evaluation and response by congregations and worship leaders based on these proposed strategies and provisional materials.

The fourth phase of the plan includes regional conferences for conversation, resource introduction and evaluation, and congregational feedback. The final phase of the process (2005 and beyond) envisions the drafting of a comprehensive proposal for new primary worship resources designed to succeed *Lutheran Book of Worship*.

As the plan progresses, the shape and parameters of that proposal will continue to unfold. The goal, however, will remain constant: renewing the worship of God in the church as it carries out Christ's mission in a new day.

Introduction

Principles for Worship presents the outcome of the first, consultative phase of Renewing Worship. During 2001, over 100 people representing the breadth of the church took part in a series of consultations that led to the formulation of these principles. *The Use of the Means of Grace,*[1] the statement on the practice of word and sacrament adopted in 1997 by the ELCA Churchwide Assembly, served as a primary foundation for this work, and is appended in this volume to the principles developed in 2001.

The consultations developed additional principles and supporting materials to address four particular dimensions of the church's worship: language, music, preaching, and worship space. These four areas represent central matters of attention for the ELCA at this time in its life; they are not, however, intended to be all-comprehensive. Like *The Use of the Means of Grace,* these additional principles, published as part of the series of Renewing Worship provisional resources, are intended to invite study and response, encourage unity, and foster common understanding and practice, rather than to impose uniformity.

The Christian Assembly
Principles for Worship is addressed to the worship of the Christian assembly, which is at the heart of the church's identity and purpose. The Lutheran confessions describe the church in terms of the worshiping assembly: "It is also taught that at all times there must be and remain one holy, Christian church. It is the assembly of all believers among whom the gospel is purely preached and the holy sacraments are administered according to the gospel."[2]

In keeping with this foundational statement, *assembly* is used consistently in *Principles for Worship* to denote the gathering of the church in worship. This word expresses well the nature of the church as *ekklesia,* a biblical word for the church that has at its root the meaning "called out." A common pattern for worship underscores this understanding of the church: The people of God are called by the Holy Spirit to *gather* around the *word of God* and the *sacraments,* so that the Spirit may in turn *send* them into the world to continue the mission of God.

Language and the Christian Assembly
One of the liveliest areas of conversation regarding worship in the church today has to do with the use of language. The ELCA is increasingly a church in which various languages,

---

[1] *The Use of the Means of Grace: A Statement on the Practice of Word and Sacrament* (Chicago: Evangelical Lutheran Church in America, 1997). This statement is reprinted as the Appendix in *Principles for Worship,* 97-143.

[2] Augsburg Confession, Article VII, *The Book of Concord,* ed. Robert Kolb and Timothy J. Wengert (Minneapolis: Fortress Press, 2000), 42. Recent English versions have used *assembly* to translate the Latin *congregatio* and the German *Versammlung.*

including but not limited to English, are used for worship. At the same time, the ongoing changes in language within the wider society have an impact on the language of worship in a church that is committed to worship in the vernacular. In addition, any discussion about language in worship is affected by the wide-ranging theological discussions about language that are taking place among Christians of many denominations and language groups.

The language section of *Principles for Worship* begins with an affirmation of the gift and purpose of human language and an acknowledgment of its limitations. Several principles on scripture and the language of worship ground the language of praise and proclamation in the Bible. The language section concludes by addressing the church's use of language in ways that reflect the unity of the church and the wide embrace of God's love, yet remain attentive to the needs of the local assembly.

Music and the Christian Assembly

The worshiping assembly uses music to proclaim and respond with gratitude to the presence and activity of the triune God in the world. Employing the resources of voices, instruments, languages, scripture, culture, and the church's witness in song through the ages, the assembly tells the story of what God has done and continues to do. The song that carries the church's prayer and lament, praise and thanksgiving to God also teaches, admonishes, inspires, and strengthens the church as it sings.

The music section of *Principles for Worship* begins by claiming music as a gift of God's creation and as a particular gift for forming and uniting God's people, especially through the primary musical expression of congregational song. In the rest of this section, the role of music in worship is articulated in several ways. Music serves the word of God and the celebration of the sacraments, even as it shapes the prayer of the assembly. Confident musical leadership invites the assembly into song and develops particular gifts among those who lead singing, play instruments, and craft music for worship. Through a rich diversity of song and other musical forms, music in worship engages the whole church and the whole person, empowering the assembly to carry out God's mission of mercy and justice in the world.

Preaching and the Christian Assembly

In a time when new forms of communication continue to emerge, preaching still holds a prominent place in the church's worship as a means of conveying the word of God. Preaching is a matter of great interest not only to those who prepare and deliver sermons week by week, but also to those who participate in preaching by listening and receiving the word, week in and week out.

The preaching section of *Principles for Worship* describes God's self-revelation as the foundation for all the ways the church proclaims God's word. Of these ways, preaching is a primary form that is essential to the church's life and an integrated part of the whole of worship. This section proceeds with a treatment of preaching as the word of God that announces law and gospel and forms people for mission, a discussion of the ministry of preaching, principles on the relationship of preaching to its context, and an exploration of the use of various communication tools in preaching.

Worship Space and the Christian Assembly

The Christian assembly gathers at particular times and in particular places. Among the central elements of worship, the place for worship is sometimes taken for granted. Yet the surroundings in which an assembly worships have the potential to shape—for good or for ill—the worship of those who gather there over many generations.

The worship space section of *Principles for Worship* articulates the close and vital relationship of worship and its space. The initial principles consider the centrality of the worshiping assembly as the foundation for building, renewing, and equipping worship spaces that enrich participation, proclaim the gospel, witness to justice, and serve the mission of God. This section then addresses primary and secondary areas within the worship space that facilitate worship and its leadership. After describing important characteristics of worship space, such as hospitality and flexibility, the section concludes with guidance for the prayerful process of building and reordering space for worship.

The Christian Assembly and Culture

When the consultative process that led to these principles was designed, it was thought that the relationship of worship and culture would be a matter for just one of the consultations, which would attend to both language and culture. It quickly became clear that the relationship of worship and culture was a critical aspect of each of the dimensions of worship being explored. Each section of *Principles for Worship,* therefore, addresses this crucial relationship. All of the consultations found a recent study on worship and culture to be especially helpful in understanding this relationship. This study is summarized here and briefly referenced within the various sections.

During the 1990's the Lutheran World Federation sponsored an international Worship and Culture Study. In its third meeting, held in Nairobi, Kenya, in January 1996, the study team developed the "Nairobi Statement on Worship and Culture: Contemporary Challenges and Opportunities."[3] This influential statement describes the relationship of worship and culture as follows.

> Christian worship relates dynamically to culture in at least four ways. First, it is *transcultural,* the same substance for everyone everywhere, beyond culture. Second, it is *contextual,* varying according to the local situation (both nature and culture). Third, it is *counter-cultural,* challenging what is contrary to the Gospel in a given culture. Fourth, it is *cross-cultural,* making possible sharing between different local cultures.[4]

Transcultural elements of worship transcend the various contexts in which assemblies gather, forming the basis for a common yet distinctive "culture of the gospel" that unites all Christians. The church's encounter with the crucified and risen Christ is at the heart of worship wherever it takes place. Central transcultural elements of worship include baptism and the eucharist, the sacraments of Christ's death and resurrection, given by God for all the world. The fundamental shape of the primary weekly gathering of Christians is transcultural: the people gather; the word of God is proclaimed and responded to in reading, preaching, song, and prayer; the eucharistic meal is shared; and the people are sent out into the world in mission.[5]

Contextual elements of worship recognize that Jesus "was born into a specific culture of the world. In the mystery of his incarnation are the model and the mandate for the contextualization of Christian worship."[6] Values, patterns, and institutions of a particular culture that are consonant with the gospel may often be used to express the meanings and actions of worship. For example, the use of a profound bow in some cultures might be parallel to

---

[3] The Nairobi Statement is published in *Christian Worship: Unity in Cultural Diversity,* ed. S. Anita Stauffer (Geneva: Lutheran World Federation, 1996), 23-28.
[4] Nairobi Statement, 1.3.
[5] Nairobi Statement, 2.1.
[6] Nairobi Statement, 3.1.

the use of a handshake in other cultures as a way of extending the greeting of peace. The basic shape of baptism—washing with water and the word of God—has been supplemented in various cultures by actions such as the giving of salt, a lighted candle, or a baptismal garment.

The *countercultural* dimension of worship recognizes that some elements of every culture in the world are sinful, dehumanizing, and contradictory to the values of the gospel. Christian faith and worship challenge all kinds of oppression, inequity, and injustice wherever they exist and where they may even be commended by earthly cultures. In addition to critiquing and transforming cultural patterns that are reflected in worship, the countercultural approach may include the intentional use of worship elements that differ from or contradict.prevailing cultural models.[7]

The *cross-cultural* dimension of worship recognizes that Christians from various cultures share worship elements with one another across cultural barriers, enriching the whole church and strengthening its awareness of the unity that is God's gift. Such sharing across ecumenical or cultural lines calls for care, integrity, and respect, motivated by a desire to welcome and enter into partnership with people of other cultures and traditions rather than merely to add a superficial variety to worship. Cross-cultural commitments can enrich the worship of any local assembly, but they are especially vital in communities that include a multiplicity of cultures.[8]

With its fourfold articulation of the critical relationship of worship and culture, the Nairobi Statement is affirmed and often presumed in *Principles for Worship*.

The Pattern of Principles for Worship

Following the pattern of *The Use of the Means of Grace*, the material in *Principles for Worship* is presented in three categories: principles, applications, and backgrounds.

Principles are brief, foundational statements that seek to articulate central understandings and practices of worship. Principles are framed so that they may form the basis for more specific applications.

Applications are specific examples of practices that may derive from the principles. Applications offer descriptive rather than prescriptive approaches to carrying out principles.

---

[7] Nairobi Statement, 4.1.
[8] Nairobi Statement, 5.1.

The applications associated with a principle illustrate one or several ways in which a principle might be applied; they are not intended to be comprehensive.

Backgrounds offer information, historical perspective, and theological rationale. Background statements may provide context and support for a principle, an application, or both. Background statements are summaries rather than exhaustive treatments of the subject matter.

Whether principle, application, or background, the statements in *Principles for Worship* are intended to encourage unity in the church while recognizing that "our congregations receive and administer the means of grace in richly diverse ways."[9] *Principles for Worship* does not seek to secure conformity or impose uniformity.

The 2001 Churchwide Consultations

Many voices from across the church have participated in developing the contents of *Principles for Worship*. Participants in four consultative groups met over a period of ten months to generate the materials. Additional reviewers from within and beyond the churchwide structure have commented and contributed to the end result.

In late 2000 a multiyear plan for the next generation of ELCA worship resources was endorsed and funded by several units of the ELCA: the Church Council, the board of the Division for Congregational Ministries (DCM), and the trustees of the Publishing House (Augsburg Fortress). Soon thereafter, participants were appointed to churchwide consultations on language, music, preaching, and worship space. Consultants were included to represent the ELCA's diverse worship practices; the divisions, commissions, seminaries, and bishops of this church; representatives from churches in full communion with the ELCA (noted in the list that follows); and resource persons from the ELCA and beyond bringing particular knowledge and background to the areas of study.

The consultations held their first meeting February 22-25, 2001, in Lisle, Illinois. Each consultation selected a chair and a writing team to work between meetings of the full consultations. Each consultation met two additional times, with the final consultation concluding its work December 1, 2001.

Between the second and third meetings of the consultations, a draft of *Principles for Worship* was presented to selected reviewers, including members of all the consultations,

---

[9] *The Use of the Means of Grace,* application 4B (see appendix).

members of the DCM board, a youth focus group assembled by the worship and youth ministries teams, and others who were asked to respond to particular theological and cultural issues. Careful consideration of responses from these reviewers became an important part of the agenda for the consultations' third and final meetings.

Between December 2001 and February 2002 the preview edition of *Principles for Worship* underwent a focused theological and liturgical review, and respondents from across the church also offered feedback to this edition, which was available on the Web. Review and feedback from these sources has been incorporated into this edition, which the board of the Division for Congregational Ministries in its February 2002 meeting received and released for distribution. This published version is also available electronically at www.renewingworship.org.

Principles for Worship is offered to the church with the hope that it will be useful to congregations, worship committees and worship leaders, pastors and other rostered professionals, colleges and seminaries, churchwide leaders, ecumenical partners, and all who have an interest in the church's worship. In addition to informing the ongoing work of Renewing Worship as new worship resources are developed for the ELCA, this document offers an opportunity for study, conversation, and response within the church about matters of worship. The principles come with high hopes from those who prepared them for a revitalization of worship, for rich conversation about these things that matter deeply in the church's life, and for clear attention to the role of worship in carrying out the mission of God in the world.

Consultation Participants

Language Consultation
Ruth A. Allin, Chicago, IL*
Kevin Anderson, Chicago, IL*‡
M. Wyvetta Bullock, Chicago, IL
Joanne Chadwick, Chicago, IL
Susan Palo Cherwien, St. Louis Park, MN*
Joseph Donnella II, Gettysburg, PA
Joanne Engquist, Cambridge, MA
Karris Golden, Waterloo, IA
Victor Jortack, Minneapolis, MN
Randall Lee, Chicago, IL
Jonathan Linman, Pittsburgh, PA
Kathryn Lohre, Somerville, MA
Charles Maahs, Shawnee Mission, KS
Madeleine Forell Marshall, Escondido, CA
Michelle Miller, Chicago, IL
Gail Ramshaw, Philadelphia, PA*
H. Frederick Reisz Jr., Columbia, SC
Robert Sandoval, Albuquerque, NM
Thomas Schattauer, Dubuque, IA*§
Frank Senn, Evanston, IL
Ann Tiemeyer, Woodside, NY
Julie Tillberg, Bethlehem, PA
Marian Wang, Naperville, IL
Arthur G. Clyde, Cleveland, OH
(United Church of Christ)
André Lavergne, New Hamburg, ON
(Evangelical Lutheran Church in Canada)
Ruth Meyers, Evanston, IL
(The Episcopal Church)
Martha Moore-Keish, Louisville, KY
(Presbyterian Church—USA)

Music Consultation
Norma Aamodt-Nelson, Minneapolis, MN
Mark Bangert, Chicago, IL
Lorraine Brugh, Valparaiso, IN*
Michael Cobbler, Chesterton, IN*
Myrna Diaz, Guayanabo, PR
Richard Erickson, New York, NY*
Handt Hanson, Burnsville, MN
Linda Kempke, Brooklyn, OH
Michael Krentz, Emmaus, PA
Fuad Nijim, Santa Clara, CA
Bonnie Olsgaard, Missoula, MT
Mary Preus, Minneapolis, MN*§
Janet Stotts, Wasilla, AK
Pedro Suarez, Aurora, Il
Richard Webb, West Des Moines, IA
Scott Weidler, Chicago, IL*‡
Paul Westermeyer, St. Paul, MN*
Todd Zielinski, Pineville, NC
Karen Johnson-Lefsrud, Victoria, BC
(Evangelical Lutheran Church in Canada)
Nola Reed Knouse, Winston-Salem, NC
(Moravian Church in America)
Teresita Valeriano, Geneva, Switzerland
(Lutheran World Federation)

Preaching Consultation
Michael L. Burk, Waverly, IA*
David Chen, San Diego, CA
Pamela Fickenscher, Minneapolis, MN*
Diane Jacobson, St. Paul, MN
Richard A. Jensen, Park Ridge, IL*§
Ivis LaRiviere-Mestre, Allentown, PA
Craig Lewis, Minneapolis, MN
Paul Lutz, Chicago, IL
Katherine S. Miller, Silver Springs, MD
Bruce Modahl, River Forest, IL
Melinda Quivik, Berkeley, CA
Robert A. Rimbo, Detroit, MI
Vance Robbins, Minneapolis, MN
Kathleen Seaton, Wayne, PA
Martin A. Seltz, Minneapolis, MN*‡
Melinda Wagner, Portland, OR
Jann Boyd, Saskatoon, SK*
(Evangelical Lutheran Church in Canada)
John Paarlberg, New York, NY
(Reformed Church in America)

Worship Space Consultation
Paul Barribeau, Cedarburg, WI*
Tanja Butler, Lynn, MA
Noralyn Carpenter, Arlington, TX*
Lori Claudio, Chicago, IL
Richard Giles, Philadelphia, PA*
Robert D. Hawkins, Columbia, SC
Walter Huffman, Columbus, OH*§
Gwendolyn King, Hanover, NH
Karen LaFollette Marohn, Columbia, SC
Christine Reinhard, Fenton, MI*
Martin Russell, Omaha, NE
Harvard Stephens, Laurel, MD
William Trexler, Norfolk, VA
Karen Ward, Chicago, IL*‡
Lawrence Haave, Delta, BC
(Evangelical Lutheran Church in Canada)

Renewing Worship Project Management Staff
Michael L. Burk, Chicago, IL*
Cheryl Dieter, Chicago, IL*
Martin A. Seltz, Minneapolis, MN*
Frank Stoldt, Chicago, IL*

Other Consultation Staff
Cartresa Hudson, Chicago, IL
Linda Parriott, Minneapolis, MN
Michael Rothaar, Chicago, IL
Mark Stahura, Minneapolis, MN
Louise Johnson, Sarah Kretzmann, Jennifer Moland-Kovash, Elizabeth Musselman, Jakob Rinderknecht, recorders

---

*   writing team
§   chair
‡   staff convener (DCM/AFP)
Geographical information reflects time of consultation appointment

Language

and the Christian Assembly

Part I: God and the Language of Worship

Language is a gift of God

Principle L-1

God is one who speaks. God calls all creation into being and gives people language as a way of responding to God and forming community.

Background L-1A

The scriptures reveal God as one who makes known the being and purpose of God. God speaks to form creation from chaos. God speaks the word of command and promise to form a people. The prophets announce "Thus says the Lord" to sound warning and to proclaim hope.

Background L-1B

Because God has woven into creation the capacity to respond, the divine word is always in dialogue. Humankind has been given the ability to respond to God through language. God calls, desiring that we answer, that we may live in communion with God.

Background L-1C

God gives language as a means through which human beings establish community with one another, interpret together the world of God's creation, and preserve over time both their stories and God's story.

Language serves the mission of God

Principle L-2

The triune God speaks in and through Christ the Word. God calls the church into being and gives us language to praise and pray, witness and serve for the life of the world.

Background L-2A

Because of sin, our age-old rebellion, the gift of language has sometimes been turned against God's purpose. We have used language to divide rather than unite, to curse rather than bless, to speak hate rather than love, to defy God rather than adore. The word that the triune God speaks to restore the world is the Word Incarnate, Jesus Christ. In worship we proclaim, "Christ has died. Christ is risen. Christ will come again." Christ is the Word who forgives sin, unites what has been divided, reconciles to God's own heart all who are estranged, and opens again our communion with God.

Application L-2B

Using language to adore and praise God, give thanks for Christ's death and resurrection, and express hope for the reign of God, the assembly celebrates the life God gives for the entire world. Using language to confess sin, cry out lament in the face of death and every evil, and intercede for the world's needs, the assembly confronts those things that oppose the abundant life God desires for all.

Application L-2C

God has entrusted us with the ministry of reconciliation. Within and beyond the worshiping assembly, we use the gift of language to carry out the mission of God—telling of God's love and faithfulness, proclaiming God's mercy and justice, and calling others to follow.

We worship in many languages

Principle L-3

The Holy Spirit creates the unity of Christ's church among persons of diverse languages as a sign of God's wide embrace. The church at worship uses many languages.

Background L-3A

The relation of the gospel and the worshiping assembly to the world's many languages and cultures is extraordinarily complex. Christian worship relates to culture in at least four ways: It is transcultural, contextual, countercultural, and cross-cultural.[10] The language of worship, as a particular instance of the interaction of worship and culture, shares in each of these four dimensions.

Application L-3B

The language of worship is transcultural. In all cultures, Christians read the scriptures in worship, wash in the water of Holy Baptism, and share in the meal of Holy Communion. The use of common texts translated into many languages identifies and binds together the worship of Christians across time and place.

Application L-3C

The language of worship is contextual. There is no single or preferred Christian sacred language. The gospel message can be proclaimed in any spoken, written, or signed language. The gospel community, the church, can be called and gathered within any culture. The church incorporates cultural expressions of various peoples into worship.

Application L-3D

The language of worship is countercultural. Praising God may be at odds with what the surrounding culture deems worthy of praise. The welcome table of the eucharist unites people whom the surrounding culture may seek to stratify and separate.

Application L-3E

The language of worship is cross-cultural. The church is gathered into one from many times and places. Certain images, concepts, and words from particular times and places cross over into other contexts within the body of Christ.

---

[10] "Nairobi Statement on Worship and Culture," in *Christian Worship: Unity in Cultural Diversity*, ed. S. Anita Stauffer (Geneva: Lutheran World Federation, 1996). See the introduction to this volume, pp. viii-x, for a fuller summary of this document.

Mercy and justice are spoken

Principle L-4

The language of worship embodies God's mercy and justice, forming us to live as merciful and just people.

Background L-4A

In words and actions the assembly encounters and proclaims the God whose justice rolls down like waters,[11] whose mercy in Christ has given us a new birth to a living hope.[12] The way language is used in worship can reflect and enact God's justice and mercy. At times, however, language in worship has been used in ways that are incongruent with the gospel message. Christians are examining the language of worship for ways in which it might demean, discriminate, or exclude, even unintentionally.

Application L-4B

The language of worship is a language of a transformed people, a foretaste of God's realm. Although all human languages are imperfect, we continually seek to use words in ways that reveal God's mercy and justice.

Application L-4C

Language used in worship has power to form and shape believers, sending us from the assembly to live as merciful and just people who serve the mission of God in this world.

Background L-4D

Many Christians are reconsidering the frequency of use of militaristic images in liturgical texts and hymns in light of Christ's mission of service, compassion, and mercy. Images that reinforce certain hierarchical views of society and the world are also being examined.

Application L-4E

Care is taken to use language that expresses mutuality with all people, all nations, and all creation, rather than attitudes of domination, division, or triumphalism.

---

[11] Amos 5:24.
[12] 1 Peter 1:3.

God is present in and yet deeper than our language

Principle L-5

God is present and acts through language. The language of worship reflects the God revealed to us and evokes the mystery of God beyond human understanding and experience.

Background L-5A

Because we cannot fully comprehend the mystery of God, the language of worship on the one hand points to and evokes the God who surpasses all understanding.[13] At the same time, God is revealed to us and gives us words to convey the very presence and grace of God. The language of worship is spoken, heard, sung, and enacted in the gathered assembly. This language, therefore, is often shaped differently from everyday conversational speech or written theological discourse.

Background L-5B

Because God is beyond the capacity of human speech fully to express, the Christian community frequently speaks about God in metaphor. Metaphor is multilayered, symbolic language that points beyond itself to a greater truth or reality. Metaphor is a deep well from which many can drink, a door open to communal meaning. Liturgical metaphor is drawn primarily from the stories and images of scripture.

Application L-5C

The language of worship is carefully crafted to convey meaning to the worshiper. Texts are composed with attention to the rhythms and resonance of speech. Well-crafted liturgical language is durable, able to bear repetition and the weight of mystery.

---

[13] Philippians 4:4.

Worship is more than words

Principle L-6

Because words alone cannot express the fullness of God, nonverbal elements of worship complement words in the vocabulary of worship.

Application L-6A
Music opens the heart and helps the community praise God and proclaim God's peace. Music unites mind, heart, and body, so that the Christian community can with one voice praise God.[14]

Application L-6B
Silence is more than a pause between other elements of worship. Silence is integral to worship, a time for the prayers of the heart, a time for listening, a time for being still in the presence of God.

Application L-6C
Actions in worship, such as gesture, ritual movement, and dance, as well as the visual and architectural environment, are significant elements of worship.[15] Sometimes these nonverbal elements communicate powerfully on their own, and sometimes they support and enhance the words that they accompany.

[14] See "Music and the Christian Assembly," 23-46.
[15] See "Worship Space and the Christian Assembly," 67-96.

Part II: Scripture and the Language of Worship

Scripture is proclaimed

Principle L-7

The reading and hearing of the scriptures is an essential part of worship and the basis for other forms of proclamation.

Background L-7A
The public reading of the scriptures is embodied and communal. People encounter the word of God in a different way when it is proclaimed to the gathered assembly than when it is read privately. Despite ongoing changes in the ways people communicate, public reading of scripture remains foundational to proclamation within the assembly. The act of reading and receiving the word is a sign of a people called and gathered by God.

Application L-7B
Training, rehearsal, and prayerful preparation assist those who read the scriptures to proclaim the word of God so that it can be clearly heard and its meaning conveyed. Attentive listening is as important to full participation in worship as is effective public reading.

Background L-7C
The Revised Common Lectionary[16] has been adopted or recommended by many church bodies worldwide. Its three-year pattern of three readings and a psalm for each occasion offers the church at worship a wide array of biblical language and imagery. The lectionary focuses on the death and resurrection of Christ as central to the meaning of the Bible for the assembly.

Application L-7D
We join an increasing number of churches worldwide in using the three-year lectionary as the primary basis for preaching, as a source of language and imagery for worship texts and hymnody, as a foundation for formation and devotional reflection, and as a sign of unity.

---

[16] For background on the Revised Common Lectionary, see the introductory material in *The Revised Common Lectionary*, prepared by the Consultation on Common Texts (Nashville: Abingdon Press, 1992).

Background L-7E

Since the first decades of the church, Christians have been translating their vocabulary and imagery from one language to another. One of Martin Luther's primary tasks was the translation of the Bible into the vernacular. Christians continue to translate the Bible into various languages.

Background L-7F

Translation from one language to another always involves some degree of interpretation and cultural adaptation. For example, the English word *love* is used to translate at least three different Greek words, and the *abba* of Jesus' native tongue is not precisely the same as the Greek *pater* or the English *father*. No translation is perfect or perfectly accurate.

Application L-7G

In worship, the biblical readings are proclaimed using a translation that is faithful to the original, appropriate to the assembly, and suitable for public reading. There is value in the consistent use of a particular translation. Many churches use the New Revised Standard Version of the Bible in their worship.

Scripture is the source of language in worship

Principle L-8

Texts used in worship are grounded in the language of the scriptures.

Background L-8A

The primary words and images of the Christian faith are rooted in the Bible. Theological and devotional reflection has sprung from this vocabulary, attempting to make it more accessible to believers in every age. The assembly uses words drawn directly from biblical translations, adaptations of scriptural language that serve a particular element of worship, and other texts that have imagery and concepts based directly on scripture.

Application L-8B

The scriptures are the source for a number of texts adapted for use in worship, such as the words of institution, the Lord's Prayer, and the Aaronic benediction. In the case of frequently used words such as these, common texts representing current ecumenical scholarship and convergence may have an advantage over other translations.

Background L-8C

Most church bodies, following Matthew 28, have baptized in the name of the Father, and of the Son, and of the Holy Spirit. "While a worldwide ecumenical discussion is now underway about such language, we have no other name in which to baptize than the historic and ecumenically received name."[17] Some churches are providing additional texts to accompany the traditional language in order to enrich the ways of expressing the meaning of the Trinity.

Application L-8D

While the text from Matthew 28 is used to accompany the threefold washing of baptism, other texts within the baptismal liturgy, such as prayers and hymns, may expand our language for the triune God.

---

[17] *Baptism, Eucharist, and Ministry. Faith and Order Paper No. 111* (Geneva: World Council of Churches, 1982), Baptism, 17, quoted in *The Use of the Means of Grace*, background 24A (see appendix).

Application L-8E

The psalms and biblical canticles have a central place in the church's prayer and song. A translation of the psalms for use in worship will reflect the fact that the psalms are poetry, faithfully rendering the Hebrew texts in contemporary language. A translation of the psalms and canticles will also attend to their singability and the accessibility of the poetry in order to enhance their use as prayer.

Background L-8F

Our experience and understanding of God can be limited by the predominant use of particular images and forms of language. For example, many people find exclusively masculine language for God a serious deterrent to their worship. Christians continue to discuss the extent to which liturgical texts drawn from the Bible should retain such terminology. Various human languages present their own respective problems and possibilities in the task of translation. Some churches are working to expand the language of worship beyond predominantly masculine words and images.

Application L-8G

Versions of biblical texts used in the liturgy, including psalms and other biblical songs, dialogues, acclamations, and blessings, may employ various strategies to render the ancient language and imagery in an expansive manner.

The treasury of language grows

Principle L-9

The church continually builds upon the vocabulary of the scriptures, expanding the treasury of language and images in order to proclaim the fullness of the triune God.

Background L-9A
Although many texts sung in worship are biblical psalms, canticles, and ancient scriptural hymn fragments, the church has also received the rich inheritance and ongoing gift of hymnody, which elaborates and complements biblical texts.

Application L-9B
The primary source of hymnody is the revelation of God in scripture and in the person of Jesus Christ. Its language is often the language of metaphor. The pairing of words with music engages the whole person and unites the assembly. Hymns are composed with great care, understanding, and respect for the gathering that sings them.

Background L-9C
Encouraged by the twentieth-century revival of the psalms, as well as the study of works of early Christian writers and poetic writings of Christian mystics, Christians in our day are reclaiming images of God that have been lost in many traditions, and they are expanding this treasury with contemporary words and images.

Background L-9D
Our addressing God as *Father* is rooted primarily in the New Testament and in the confessions and piety of the church. Our use of this form of address is related in part to Jesus' invitation to join him in praying to God in this way. This form of address has become more prevalent in the last two centuries, sometimes overshadowing other ways of addressing God.

Background L-9E
Lord is cherished by many as a direct address for God. This masculine title became a substitute for YHWH (one translation for which is *I Am*), the name ascribed to God in the Hebrew scriptures that, out of reverence, was customarily not spoken aloud. Early Christian confessions identified Jesus as Lord. Currently, churches and individuals are exploring other words and images to complement the use of *Lord*.

Application L-9F
The rich biblical language for God includes numerous ways of addressing God, uses both female and male images, and employs social and natural metaphors to describe and call upon God. Varied images and ways of addressing God help the assembly envision the fullness of the Trinity.

Application L-9G
Careful crafting of texts to minimize the use of gender-specific pronouns for God helps to avoid conveying the impression that God is either male or female.

Application L-9H
Worshipers' familiarity with scripture varies. To assist all to participate fully in the richness of worship, biblical speech and metaphors may require explanation and interpretation. Bible study outside the liturgy complements proclamation within the liturgy.

Part III: The Church and the Language of Worship

Worship is participatory

Principle L-10

Worship involves all those who gather. Many voices share in the language of worship, taking various roles.

Background L-10A
Christians believe that the triune God is both One and Three-in-One, that within the very unity of God there is also the dynamic of relationship and community. The communal participation of all in the assembly is a reflection of the communal life of the triune God into whom we have been baptized.

Application L-10B
People may participate more vigorously when they know the words by heart or can readily repeat what they hear. When introduced with care, new texts that are suitable for assembly use can be added to the treasury of memorable texts.

Application L-10C
The language of the liturgy is spoken, sung, signed, and embodied in action by the assembly. Undue reliance on the reading of worship materials by the assembly and its leaders can inhibit engagement in worship. Worship resources for use in the assembly best fulfill their goal when they facilitate participation rather than dependence.

Application L-10D
A growing number of communities include people with different primary languages. To encourage full participation of those present at worship, several languages or a language held in common may be used within a given liturgy. The assembly may sing, speak, and/or sign together in more than one language at the same time. Texts may be spoken in one language with translation provided in a worship folder or in some other way that facilitates the flow of the liturgy. The liturgical action alone can reveal the meaning of some common texts.

Application L-10E
Local communities may make use of culturally specific idioms and acclamations as resources for building up the body of Christ. Worship may include verbal feedback, shout, and ecstatic utterance. Interjections such as "Have mercy, Jesus" and "Amen" are expressions of participation rather than interruptions.

The language of worship is both ordinary and extraordinary

Principle L-11

The language of worship uses carefully crafted vernacular speech as well as words and expressions not common in everyday speech.

Background L-11A

Christians share some common vocabulary taken from the original languages of the Bible and the Christian tradition. In their assemblies Christians continue to use the Hebrew words *hallelujah* and *amen*. Some assemblies retain the Greek prayer *Kyrie eleison,* and some find helpful the use of Latin, such as *Gloria in excelsis Deo.* Some texts may be devotionally powerful in widely memorized forms that use older language idioms.

Application L-11B

Although vernacular language is the primary language used in worship, certain non-vernacular terms and expressions integral to the vocabulary of Christian faith and tradition enrich our worship by linking the assembly to God's people across time and space.

Application L-11C

In some Christian assemblies, public worship includes speaking in tongues.[18] Whether this practice is personally expressive or serves as proclamation, in which case interpretation is provided for the assembly, it is intended for the edification and unity of the worshiping community.[19]

---

[18] Acts 10:44-48, Acts 19:5-6, Romans 8:26, 1 Corinthians 12:10.
[19] 1 Corinthians 14.

Common texts are a sign of unity

Principle L-12

The use of texts held in common is a sign of the communion of the church across time and space.

Background L-12A

The worship resources of the church include historic texts from a variety of traditions. Ecumenical cooperation in recent decades has produced a body of common English translations of historic liturgical texts, the three-year lectionary, and some convergence on a common core of hymn texts.[20]

Application L-12B

We seek to acknowledge and develop liturgical texts and hymns in cooperation with other churches. We support and participate in ecumenical efforts to prepare texts for common use, and initiate such cooperation where none exists. This church may also adopt or adapt texts prepared for use in other churches.

Application L-12C

Some texts and hymns are shared within a confessional or liturgical tradition. The use of common texts in a particular tradition serves its distinctive witness, preserves treasures of faith for generations to come, and offers gifts to the wider church.

---

[20] The International Consultation on English Texts, the Consultation on Ecumenical Hymnody, the Consultation on Common Texts (North America), and the English Language Liturgical Consultation represent the ecumenical effort among many English-speaking churches to find common words for Christian worship. In addition to the work of these ecumenical working groups, texts produced for use within a particular church body are often shared more broadly. Examples include the wide dissemination of texts prepared by the International Committee on English in the Liturgy (Roman Catholic) and of texts found in the *Book of Common Prayer*, 1979 (Episcopal) and *Lutheran Book of Worship*, 1978. In earlier times, Lutheran immigrant churches in North America regularly looked to the prayer book tradition of the Episcopal Church for English-language liturgical texts.

Ecumenical creeds are a sign of unity

Principle L-13

The ecumenical creeds used in worship confess the faith of the church through the ages and around the world.

Background L-13A

A creed is a statement of faith of the whole church. The three ecumenical creeds in use at this time are the Apostles' Creed, the Nicene Creed, and the Athanasian Creed. Some congregations and church bodies are experimenting with new statements of belief.

Application L-13B

Because every congregation's worship is open to the whole church, the ecumenical creeds are the creeds used in worship, unless and until a worldwide ecumenical consensus is reached regarding additional creedal texts. Eucharistic prayers and trinitarian hymns are confessions of faith that complement the ecumenical creeds.

Memory and faith shape and sustain each other

Principle L-14

The language of worship nourishes the memory of the community and the individual. Both repeating familiar texts and taking to heart memorable new texts sustain faith across generations.

Background L-14A
Our memories, our experience of language, and our Christian faith are intricately related. We remember the scriptures, prayers, and hymns used in worship as powerful representations of shared experience and for their personal associations. Recollected language is deeply intertwined with the collective history of Christian faith through the ages and with the individual experience of faith.

Background L-14B
Frequently repeated texts enter the long-term memory of individuals and communities. These texts are often known by heart, providing solace in times of upheaval and loss, offering a means of expression in moments of celebration and joy. The language learned in worship can comfort and support each of us at critical times in life and when nearing death.

Application L-14C
Over time, each community of faith develops a body of hymns, prayers, and liturgical texts that are connected to the broader church and that are familiar or even known by heart. Incorporating worthy unknown and new texts into the memory of the community enriches faith.

Application L-14D
One way to connect with the broader church is to keep alive the words of the faithful departed. We worship using the texts they wrote; for example, the prayers and hymns of Francis of Assisi.[21] Selections from writings of or about the faithful departed may be read at morning and evening prayer, especially on their commemoration days.

---

[21] See "A Prayer Attributed to St. Francis" and "All Creatures of Our God and King," in *LBW*, page 48 and hymn 527.

Application L-14E
Care is taken in adapting, altering, or replacing texts, so as to respect the memory of the community and the witness of previous generations.

Background L-14F
Because the language of worship evolves to reflect changes in language and in the articulation of the faith, those who have been absent for an extended period of time may find that some of the words of worship are unfamiliar. The assembly may also include those whose experience of Christian worship is limited or different from the practice of the assembly.

Application L-14G
The community hospitably assists those new or returning to the assembly, accompanies them in worship as they learn traditions, customs, language, and music unfamiliar to them, and nurtures their understanding and sense of belonging.

The language of worship embraces all

Principle L-15

The language of worship reflects God's love for all creation. We seek to use words, images, and metaphors that express the breadth of God's love.

Background L-15A
The language of worship invites us to see the world from the perspective of God, to envision the world in a larger way and strive to discern God's purpose at work within it. Words, images, and metaphors used in worship are always being reevaluated as the world changes and according to our discernment of God's purpose for the world.

Application L-15B
The language of worship reflects God's love for people of every color and ethnicity. Discernment is needed in evaluating texts that use color terms metaphorically.

Application L-15C
The language of worship reflects God's love for all persons regardless of gender. The use of nongendered terms for people, as reflected, for example, in most current North American English language style guidelines, is a preferred practice for the words of worship.

Application L-15D
The language of worship reflects God's love for people of differing abilities. Texts and directions attend to the diversity of physical abilities and other capacities.

Application L-15E
The language of worship reflects God's love for people of all ages and varied human experiences. Language used in worship avoids preference for one group over another.

Application L-15F
The language of worship reflects God's love for the whole creation. The words of worship express our respect and care for all that God has made.

Language in the local assembly

Principle L-16

Words appropriate to the local context characterize certain parts of the liturgy.

Background L-16A
The pattern for Christian worship includes not only fixed texts but also opportunities for local expression, particularly the sermon and the intercessions.

Application L-16B
The prayers of intercession convey to God our lament, our hope, and our thanksgiving. These prayers are formulated locally for each occasion and are carefully crafted to reflect the wideness of God's mercy for the whole world.

Application L-16C
The preparation and leading of the intercessions by a lay assisting minister is a sign that the task of praying for the world belongs to all baptized persons.

Background L-16D
In one classic pattern for the prayers of intercession, the local gathering prays for the whole church, the nations, those in need, and the congregation; includes any special concerns; and remembers the faithful departed. A recent suggested addition is a prayer for the earth.

Background L-16E
The prayers of intercession may be formulated as bids inviting the assembly's prayer, as prayers addressed to God, or in a way that combines both bids and prayers, as in the solemn prayers of intercession on Good Friday.

Application L-16F
Clarity of form and repeated use of a pattern for intercessions are helpful in guiding the minds of all who pray.

Application L-16G
Leaders of prayer present petitions that can be understood by the whole congregation. The entire assembly should be able to assent to the prayers that are offered on its behalf. The wording of petitions makes clear that these prayers are intercession addressed to God, rather than proclamation or information addressed to the people.

Application L-16H

The sermon is prepared specifically for the occasion.[22] The preaching of the crucified and risen Christ is grounded in the language of the Bible, the liturgy, and the tradition of faith. Preaching uses contemporary language to proclaim the timeless gospel in a particular context.

Application L-16I

Occasionally directions, explanations, or announcements are needed to assist the smooth flow of the assembly's worship. Care is taken that any necessary directions, explanations, or announcements are worded clearly and succinctly and are delivered at an appropriate time and in a fitting manner. Sometimes gesture can replace verbal direction.

---

[22] See "Preaching and the Christian Assembly," 47-66.

Music

and the Christian Assembly

Part I: The Nature of Music

Music is from God

Principle M-1

God creates music as part of the whole creation and gives it to humankind to develop and shape.

Background M-1A
Sound and rhythm are primal forces in creation. "God saw everything that he had made, and indeed, it was very good."[23] "When I laid the foundation of the earth . . . the morning stars sang together and all the heavenly beings shouted for joy."[24]

Background M-1B
In the first chapter of the Bible we hear how God gives human beings the gift and responsibility of forming creation, which includes music. "Let us make humankind in our image, according to our likeness; and let them have dominion . . . over . . . all the earth."[25]

Background M-1C
In and through music we recognize and respond to our creator. Martin Luther commended music as an "excellent gift of God": "From the beginning of the world it has been instilled and implanted in all creatures, individually and collectively. For nothing is without sound and harmony. . . . Let this noble, wholesome, and cheerful creation of God be commended to you. . . . At the same time you may by this creation accustom yourself to recognize and praise the Creator."[26]

---

[23] Genesis 1:31.
[24] Job 38:4, 7.
[25] Genesis 1:26.
[26] Martin Luther, "Preface to Georg Rhau's Symphoniae iucundae," in *Luther's Works*, Volume 53 (Philadelphia: Fortress Press, 1965), 321, 322, 324.

Background M-1D

Luther also affirmed the work of musicians in shaping the gift of music. He wanted to "see all the arts, especially music, used in the service of [God] who gave and made them."[27]

Application M-1E

God's gift of music is received and shaped by people into many varieties and forms, which have an important and delightful place in the worship of God.

---

[27] Martin Luther, "Preface to the Wittenberg Hymnal," in *Luther's Works*, Volume 53, 316.

The voice is the primary instrument in worship

Principle M-2

In the church, the primary musical instrument is the human voice, given by God to sing and proclaim the word of God.

Background M-2A
Scripture speaks of Jesus Christ as the incarnate Word of God. "In the beginning was the Word, and the Word was with God, and the Word was God."[28] "Let the word of Christ dwell in you richly . . . and with gratitude in your hearts sing psalms, hymns, and spiritual songs to God."[29]

Background M-2B
Luther extolled the gift of the voice: "Compared to the human voice, all [other music found in nature] hardly deserves the name of music, so abundant and incomprehensible is here the munificence and wisdom of our gracious Creator. . . . No two [people] can be found with exactly the same voice."[30]

Background M-2C
"That music comes from the *auricularia*, i.e., from the sphere of miraculous audible things—like the Gospel, that it is a unique gift of God's creation which comes to us in the same way the Word of God does, namely, mediated by the voice, that is a point at which Luther is lost in wonder again and again."[31]

Background M-2D
"Singing is a natural thing. A baby and its nursing mother do it unselfconsciously. The one goo-goos multisyllabic nonsense, while the other lah-lahs in the hope of soothing the crying one or encouraging sleep."[32]

Application M-2E
The use of the human voice is basic to communal worship. Christian proclamation is based on spoken, sung, and heard words that bear the Word Incarnate. This dialogue is continuous in worship, among worship leaders, choir, and the whole assembly.

---

[28] John 1:1.
[29] Colossians 3:16.
[30] Martin Luther, "Preface to Georg Rhau's Symphoniae iucundae," in *Luther's Works*, Volume 53, 322-24.
[31] Oskar Söhngen, "Fundamental Considerations for a Theology of Music," in *The Musical Heritage of the Church* (St. Louis: Concordia Publishing House, 1963), 15-16.
[32] John L. Bell, *The Singing Thing* (Chicago: GIA Publications, 2000), 13-14.

Application M-2F

Regardless of musical style or instrumentation, leadership confidently supports and enables the voice of the congregation. Likewise, the voice of a soloist, cantor, assisting minister, or presiding minister is most effective when it does not overwhelm or dominate the congregation's voice.

Application M-2G

The unaccompanied voice may be used for teaching and leading an assembly in song.

Application M-2H

Speaking and singing are oral and aural phenomena. In assemblies where some people do not hear or speak, sensitivity to the use of other senses in proclaiming and receiving God's word is crucial.

The assembly's song is central

Principle M-3

Music is a communal and relational activity. The assembly is the primary musical ensemble, and its song is the core of all music in worship.

Background M-3A
The assembly, though made up of many individual voices, sings in one voice. It "participates in proclaiming the Word of God with a common voice. It sings hymns and the texts of the liturgy."[33]

Background M-3B
The gathered assembly not only sings in one voice, but its song is added to the song of the church throughout the world and throughout the ages. In *Life Together* Dietrich Bonhoeffer wrote, "It is the voice of the church that is heard in singing together. It is not I who sing, but the church. However, as a member of the church, I may share in its song."[34]

Application M-3C
The gathered assembly shares in making music through the singing of hymns, songs, refrains, choruses, responses, and other liturgical music. Music-making in the assembly invites all who are present to take part, regardless of age or musical ability.

Application M-3D
Worship is enriched when worship leaders consider and account for the experience and history of the people gathered; the nature and size of the gathering; the characteristics of the space; the musical skill of the assembly and its leaders; the instrumental and vocal resources that are available; and the relationship of music to the texts.

Application M-3E
Sufficient resources of time, energy, and money are needed to support the ministry of music in a community of faith.

Application M-3F
The acoustics of a room and the physical arrangement of the assembly are best suited for worship when they contribute to the vitality of a congregation's song.

---

[33] *The Use of the Means of Grace*, principle 10 (see appendix).
[34] Dietrich Bonhoeffer, *Life Together* (Minneapolis: Fortress Press, 1996), 68.

Musical expression is varied

Principle M-4

A healthy tension between simple and complex music enriches the worshiping assembly.

Background M-4A

Referring to folk music as simple and art music as complex, while reflecting a desire to describe variety in form, is a limited expression of the breadth and richness of each. Functional music has long been welcomed and balanced with music that has proven to be more lasting.

Background M-4B

Lutheran Book of Worship is prefaced with this encouragement: "Freedom and flexibility in worship is a Lutheran inheritance, and there is room for ample variety in ceremony, music, and liturgical form."[35]

Application M-4C

An openness to diverse musical expressions allows for various musical repertoires and forms within worship. These may include chorales, folk tunes, oratorios, chorale preludes, praise choruses, liturgical settings, spiritual songs, hymns, cantatas, anthems, motets, toccatas, organ preludes and postludes, and numerous other types of music for voices and for instruments.

Application M-4D

Just as there is a wide variety in styles and forms in the music of worship, so also there is variety in the levels and ways people participate in music. At times, all participate actively in the music-making event, as in congregational singing. At other times, the congregation participates by responding, as in call and response forms or responsive refrains. At still other times, most of the people may participate by actively listening, as in a choral anthem or organ voluntary.

---

[35] Introduction, *LBW,* 8.

Assembly song forms memory and nurtures faith

Principle M-5

The assembly's song contributes to the spiritual formation of the assembly itself and its individual members. Used carefully and consistently over time, the song forms communal and individual memory and serves to nurture the faith from one generation to another.

Background M-5A
Through the songs sung in worship, God's people, including children and those new to the faith, learn their language about God and the story of salvation. These songs remain with people through life, persist when other memory fades, give meaning in later life, and are a comfort in death. In addition, congregational song handed on across time and place links the memory of individuals and particular communities to the longer corporate memory of the church.

Application M-5B
Music forms faith and memory when a healthy balance is maintained between new songs and an established core of music that is repeated. Just as repetition is a useful technique in musical composition, it is also valuable for a worshiping community. The rhythms of the church year and the liturgy itself call for a core of music that does not change constantly, but is integral to the patterns of worship. New songs are also essential to the life-long work of faith formation. As new songs are introduced in worship, God's Spirit continues to open and shape lives.

Application M-5C
Planning music for worship calls for careful attention to the people's memory. It is important that a congregation's repertoire include music of lasting value and durability so that it can bear repeated use and remain vital in the life of the congregation.

Application M-5D
People of all ages benefit when music is woven into the ministry of education. Choral programs and schools, instrumental ensembles, confirmation and Christian education programs all offer opportunities to use music in teaching the faith.

Application M-5E
Singing the church's song in the home is encouraged. Children, youth, and younger and older adults can sing with one another in various settings: prayers at meals and bedtimes, birthdays or anniversaries, and social occasions (as when Christmas carols are sung). Instruments may or may not accompany the singing.

Music involves the whole person

Principle M-6

We worship God with our bodies, through singing, movement, dance, and gesture.

Background M-6A
Movement has been an expression of worship since early biblical times.[36] Processions, standing to sing, gestures for prayer, the presenting and receiving of bread and wine, and forms of dance have historically been part of Christian worship. Music is integral to these movements.

Background M-6B
Movement in worship has varied from culture to culture. In some settings, rhythmic clapping and stomping have accompanied song. In other settings, moving and dancing have occurred. In still others, rhythmic motion has been less obvious, but attention has been given to actions such as kneeling, making the sign of the cross, or bowing.[37]

Background M-6C
In some cultures, movement and song are so closely linked that in worship the assembly's singing is typically accompanied by movement or dance. "Human community expresses the impact of the universe upon it [in] three fundamental forms . . . : dance (unity of mime and rhythm), poetry (unity of rhythm and recitation), and music (unity of rhythm and melody). The poetry and music are usually accompanied by the dance in most African communities. This link between music and dance is not limited to Africa."[38]

Application M-6D
Acceptance and understanding of gestures, postures, movement, and dance in worship may be strengthened when the assembly is prepared in advance.

---

[36] Exodus 15:20, 21.
[37] Elochukwu E. Uzukwu, *Worship as Body Language* (Collegeville: The Liturgical Press, 1997).
[38] *Worship as Body Language*, 6, 30.

Part II: Music Serves and Shapes

Music serves the word of God

Principle M-7

Music serves the word of God by bearing it in audible patterns and forms. Music proclaims and illuminates God's word, helping it resonate in the hearts and memory of the community and the individual.

Background M-7A
"The gift of language combined with the gift of song was only given to [human beings] to let [them] know that [they] should praise God with both word and music, namely, by proclaiming [God's word] through music and by providing sweet melodies with words."[39]

Background M-7B
Psalms, hymns and spiritual songs give voice to the assembly. "Our plan is to follow the example of the prophets and the ancient fathers of the church, and to compose psalms for the people [in the] vernacular, that is, spiritual songs, so that the Word of God may be among the people also in the form of music."[40]

Background M-7C
"The assembled congregation participates in proclaiming the Word of God with a common voice. It sings hymns and the texts of the liturgy."[41] "Music, the visual arts, and the environment of our worship spaces embody the proclamation of the Word in Lutheran churches."[42]

Application M-7D
The psalms, biblical canticles, and some portions of scripture are inherently musical and are intended to be sung.

---

[39] Martin Luther, "Preface to Georg Rhau's Symphoniae iucundae," in *Luther's Works,* Volume 53, 323-324.
[40] Martin Luther, "Letter to George Spalatin," in *Luther's Works,* Volume 49 (Philadelphia: Fortress Press, 1972), 68.
[41] *The Use of the Means of Grace,* principle 10 (see appendix).
[42] *The Use of the Means of Grace,* principle 11 (see appendix).

Application M-7E

Music that relates to biblical readings organized across the church year is a central way of proclaiming the word of God in worship.

Application M-7F

Singing the hymn of the day is a historically Lutheran practice with a continuing vitality that is a witness to the whole church. Since the Reformation, this hymn has served to proclaim the word, teach the faith, and keep alive a rich body of hymns from many times and places. The hymn of the day is intimately related to the texts and themes of the day and the church year. This practice invites the church to explore a breadth of choices, congregations to develop their repertoires, and musicians to employ creativity in the ways in which the hymn of the day is sung.

Music serves the sacraments

Principle M-8

Music surrounds and serves the celebration of the sacraments. As part of God's creation renewed in Christ, the people of God sing around the elements, words, and actions that bear God's grace.

Background M-8A
Various hymns, songs, and acclamations reinforce themes of baptism and are suggested for use within the baptismal rite. "While a baptismal hymn is sung, the candidates, sponsors, and parents gather at the font."[43]

Background M-8B
In the liturgy of Holy Communion "we gather in song and prayer."[44] "With Mary Magdalene and Peter and all the witnesses of the resurrection, with earth and sea and all their creatures, and with angels and archangels, cherubim and seraphim, we praise your name and join their unending hymn: Holy, holy, holy Lord, God of power and might."[45]

Application M-8C
God is present in worship. Through music the assembly seeks to praise God, proclaim the word, pray, and retell the story of what God has done and continues to do. Music gives shape to ritual action, expresses and forms faith, gathers individuals into community, and scatters them as witnesses in the world.

Application M-8D
Through our music-making in worship we invite the Holy Spirit to come and be present among us, and we are not surprised when musical moments become extraordinary.

Application M-8E
In Jesus Christ, God has taken on human nature, embracing both life and death. In worship, Jesus Christ comes in the presence of the gathered assembly, in the gifts of bread, wine, and the water of baptism. Music-making surrounds the assembly and these gifts, uplifting the grace they offer.

---

[43] Holy Baptism, *LBW*, 121.
[44] *The Use of the Means of Grace,* application 34B (see appendix).
[45] Easter preface and Sanctus, *LBW* Ministers Edition, 213.

Application M-8F

The vast repertoire of diverse music available to the church can be embraced with integrity when carefully integrated into the patterns of worship. Preludes, hymns, settings of the Kyrie and Gloria, psalms, verses, anthems, prayer responses, settings of the Sanctus and Agnus Dei, postludes, canticles, and other pieces all find a suitable place.

Music shapes and surrounds prayer

Principle M-9

Music in worship carries the assembly's prayer beyond words alone. Music shapes, nurtures, and assists the prayer of God's people.

Background M-9A

Praise and lamentation naturally lead into song, since words alone cannot fully carry laughter and sorrow. Congregational responses like "Hear our prayer" have melodic and rhythmic shape.

Application M-9B

We seek to use as fully as possible music's ability to carry prayer, allowing prayer to find expression in its natural musical shape and flow, both with words and without words. The sung prayer of the ecumenical community of Taizé is an example. Careful thought and preparation stir the winds of creativity and strengthen the assembly's prayer.

Application M-9C

The daily offices of morning and evening prayer include a vast repertoire and give opportunity for musical expressions that are cherished and nurtured by the church. Psalms and biblical canticles are especially significant. Prayer at the close of the day and other services offer additional opportunities for music at prayer.

Part III: Music Supports and Leads

The assembly is led in song

Principle M-10

The singing assembly requires leadership.

Background M-10A

From biblical times onward people have been designated to lead the service of song in God's house. "They ministered with song before the tabernacle of the tent of meeting, until Solomon had built the house of the LORD in Jerusalem; and they performed their service in due order."[46]

Background M-10B

Lutheran congregations in North America have employed a variety of titles for musicians serving the church, including director of music, minister of music, organist, choirmaster, choir director, song leader, and cantor. Whatever the title, leading the people's song is a distinct and necessary ministry within the worshiping assembly. Whether professional or volunteer, full-time or part-time, paid or unpaid, leadership of the assembly's music is a vocation.

Background M-10C

Some congregations are renewing the use of the title cantor for musicians whose vocation is to serve the church. "*Cantor* comes from the Latin word *cantare* or *canere*, which means to sing. It refers to the chief singer, the person who leads the people in singing."[47] Among Lutherans the term has been used for those who lead the assembly and its various choral and instrumental groups.[48]

Application M-10D

The responsibilities of church musicians may include gathering and managing the resources for leading the assembly's song; mentoring the young and those new to the faith; forming and educating the faithful; planning music for liturgies; leading the prayer of the assembly; training choirs, instrumental groups, and individuals of all ages; and developing concerts and other outreach programs.

---

[46] 1 Chronicles 6:32.
[47] Paul Westermeyer, *The Church Musician* (Minneapolis: Augsburg Fortress, 1997), 13.
[48] "The Role of the Cantor" (Association of Lutheran Church Musicians Standing Committee on Ministry, 1989).

Application M-10E

Those who lead the people's song are encouraged to lead with confidence and skill. Participation by the assembly in its song is deepened when musical leadership is supported by lives of prayer and reflection, study and practice.

Application M-10F

The church supports and nurtures people who are called by God to the vocation of church musician. Educational opportunities for church musicians are offered through various colleges, universities, seminaries, camps, and other institutions within and beyond the church. Financial support for the training and continuing education of present and future church musicians is a responsibility of congregations. Congregations also provide fair compensation and just treatment for church musicians, regularly evaluating and examining expectations for music positions.

Application M-10G

Although various patterns exist for the relationship of various ministries in the church, musicians work best in partnership and mutual ministry with pastors and other leaders. Such collegiality, developed through models such as mentoring, benefits those who serve in these various roles and, through their cooperative ministry, the church.

Application M-10H

Church musicians also live out their vocation by being involved in the wider ministry of the church locally and through participation in synodical, churchwide, and ecumenical events. Outreach, education, and all aspects of mission are strengthened by the involvement of church musicians.

The choir serves the assembly

Principle M-11

Choirs lead, teach, and proclaim within the assembly.

Background M-11A
Choirs may be large or small, may meet regularly or occasionally, and may include adults, youth, or children in various combinations.

Background M-11B
"In the Lutheran tradition of worship the choir . . . supports and enriches . . . congregational singing, . . . [sings] the portions of the liturgy entrusted to it, . . . [and presents] attendant music as appropriate and possible [as in] motets, anthems, Passions, cantatas, and other music."[49]

Background M-11C
J. S. Bach, whose cantatas for vocal and instrumental ensembles make up the largest part of his output, "understood his art in terms of proclamation of the word," and said in connection with 2 Chronicles 5:13, "Where there is devotional music, God with . . . grace is always present."[50]

Application M-11D
The choir rehearses the assembly's music to lead it, sings music beyond the congregation's capacity, and serves responsively in alternation with the congregation. The principles of congregational song apply to choirs. Choral music bears a relationship to the texts for the day, the season of the church year, and the context for which it is planned. Leaders take into account the abilities and needs of the choir and the congregation in choosing music for the choir. Development of choral singing can enliven and strengthen singing of the assembly.

Application M-11E
Small vocal ensembles, instrumental ensembles, and soloists can play an important role in the assembly. Inviting and using the gifts present in the community broadens and enriches opportunities for musical leadership.

---

[49] Carl Halter and Carl Schalk, eds., *A Handbook of Church Music* (St. Louis: Concordia Publishing House, 1978), 19, 21.
[50] Robin Leaver, ed., *J. S. Bach and Scripture* (St. Louis: Concordia Publishing House, 1985), 93, 97.

Instruments and technology are used with care

Principle M-12

Choices concerning the use of technology and instrumentation in worship are informed by the priority that is placed on congregational song.

Background M-12A
In the western church prior to the Reformation, in the Lutheran church during and after the Reformation, and in most western Christian churches for the last several hundred years, instruments have been employed in worship. During this time the pipe organ emerged as the primary musical instrument for Christian worship. This is partially because of the organ's ability to sustain tones, to fill large spaces with sound, and to produce sound the way the human voice does by air vibrating in pipes. The pipe organ has garnered a large musical repertoire associated with the church. In other cultures the drum, with its relationship to the heartbeat, has held a similar status.

Background M-12B
The church has not always used instruments in worship. Early Christian churches largely rejected them as associated with immorality and idolatry; the eastern church still does not use them; and Calvinists at the time of the Reformation and for some time thereafter did not use them.

Application M-12C
Assemblies make the best use of the musical instruments available to them. Depending on the context, the worship space, and the styles of music, instruments including organs, pianos, keyboards, drums, guitars, and many others can be used effectively to lead congregational song.

Application M-12D
The living voice of the gospel is proclaimed with integrity through music that is live: that is, music led by people present in the assembly, music that uplifts the primacy of the assembly's voice, and music that avoids the use of technology to replace human leadership and participation.

Application M-12E

Worshiping communities are encouraged to make use of the entire dynamic spectrum, including silence. Organs, synthesizers, drums, and other instruments make possible far louder sounds than any assembly can produce through singing. While louder sound levels are typical in some genres of music, care for ears and voices encourages appropriate and sensitive choices regarding the decibel level of music.

Application M-12F

In every congregation and community, regardless of size or resources, God gives people the capacity for musical expression in worship. The gathering and use of these gifts may require creative choices and reframed expectations. Music for the worship of God can be full and complete using unaccompanied singing, indigenous instrumentation, and simple repertoire.

Music is well-crafted

Principle M-13

Those who plan, compose, lead, and make music are called upon to offer their very best to God and the assembly.

Background M-13A

Music as the living voice of the gospel leads to the finest craft. "It faithfully reflects in its own terms the honesty, integrity, truthfulness, and winsomeness of the Gospel message. . . . To view music as gift and creation of God . . . has implications for the craft of music and the integrity of musical composition . . . its fitness . . . suitability . . . [and] 'well-madeness' *as music*."[51]

Application M-13B

Musicians serving the church combine a desire to glorify God and to build up the community with a commitment to musical proficiency. The assembly and its song are strengthened when music is thoughtfully chosen, carefully prepared, and beautifully rendered in a manner suitable to its style and the context in which it is presented.

Application M-13C

No matter the size of a congregation, financial resources available, or the skills of the musician, each assembly can seek excellent musical expression appropriate and honest to its own context.

Application M-13D

The crafts of composition, improvisation, appropriate performance practice, and excellence in building and maintaining of instruments are encouraged.

Application M-13E

Music for weddings, funerals, and other rites of passage is worthy of the same attention as music for the primary gatherings of the Christian assembly.

---

[51] Carl Schalk, *Luther on Music* (St. Louis: Concordia Publishing House, 1988), 51.

Part IV: Music Restores and Connects

Music serves the unity of the church

Principle M-14

The church's song embraces traditions from other times and places throughout the world as well as the particularity of a specific congregation in one time and place.

Background M-14A

Our unity in Christ is reflected in our witness in music throughout the centuries and throughout the world. We stand at this end of a great procession of believers who have responded with gratitude to the presence and activity of the triune God, and we are stewards of a great progression of musical wisdom from a host of cultures and churches who confess Christ. "We are united in one common center: Jesus Christ proclaimed in Word and sacraments amidst participating assemblies of singing, serving, and praying people."[52]

Application M-14B

Worship is strengthened when music spans the generations and honors the faithfulness of people in a variety of locales. A rich and varied set of songs guards against a tendency to reflect a limited view of God, ourselves, and the church.

Application M-14C

In communion with partners from around the world (for instance, the Lutheran World Federation and the World Council of Churches), this church is open to a broad perspective of resources for worship.

Application M-14D

Although the repertoire of song will vary from one worshiping community to another depending on a number of contextual factors, there is value in identifying and developing a common core of song that unites various worshiping assemblies within a congregation, and in turn unites those assemblies with the church at large.

---

[52] *The Use of the Means of Grace,* application 4B (see appendix).

Music expresses cultural diversity

Principle M-15

Music of many cultures, revealing the wonder of creation in its great variety, is available for use in worship.

Background M-15A
"Christian worship relates dynamically to the culture in at least four ways. . . . It is transcultural, . . . contextual, . . . counter-cultural, . . . [and] cross-cultural."[53]

Background M-15B
God's word is an oral and enfleshed event that seeks a voice, longing for expression in song, hymn, or dance. As these musical possibilities take shape within the world's cultures, a colorful array of musical possibilities emerges.[54]

Background M-15C
The church has always shared and adapted music across cultures. Because meaning in music is experienced through a cultural lens, the transmission of music across cultural borders produces adaptation and modification. Many types of relationships can develop from such sharing. This sharing may result in a growing awareness of both the unity and diversity of the body of Christ.

Application M-15D
A respect for other cultures is crucial when using music that arises from outside one's own cultural context. An informed use of music from another culture will include learning what one can about techniques, Background, and history of that music and its people. Such a use can never replicate the original context, but seeks to find an authentic expression in the gathered assembly in which it finds itself. Music for worship honors and includes gifts arising from the global body of Christ, including music from historic western traditions as well as the emerging music of new composers from every part of the earth.

Application M-15E
In some worshiping communities, music written within the community itself for local use may be appropriate. The breadth of the church is expressed when local music is balanced with music from other expressions of the church.

---

[53] "Nairobi Statement on Worship and Culture" in *Christian Worship: Unity in Cultural Diversity*, ed. S. Anita Stauffer (Geneva: Lutheran World Federation, 1996), 1.3. See the introduction to this volume, pp. viii-x, for a fuller summary of this document.
[54] Mark P. Bangert, "Dynamics of Liturgy and World Musics" in *Worship and Culture in Dialogue,* ed. S. Anita Stauffer (Geneva: Lutheran World Federation, 1994), 189.

Music is related to healing and wholeness

Principle M-16

Music engages the whole community and the whole person.

Background M-16A
Music draws people together, making connections on many levels—spiritual, physical, social, emotional, and intellectual. The whole community and the individuals within it are moved to respond. "Let everything that breathes praise the Lord!"[55]

Background M-16B
"Imagine your church members filling their space at the beginning of the liturgy. Imagine that all the space in the room is full of the possibility of song. . . . The amazing thing is that this can happen every time we sing. . . . We are literally 'one body' when we sing together in this way. One with each other, one with the physical universe, and one with the Creator who gave us the Song."[56]

Background M-16C
In its wholeness, a community remembers and sings for those who are absent or unable to sing, including those who have been silenced by abuse, racism, sexism, homophobia, mental illness, violence, tragedy, or any form of exclusion.

Application M-16D
Music can be a means of healing and reconciliation. By the power of God's Spirit, music can encourage and sustain health. By bringing to voice the needs for healing, the community is called to forgiveness and reconciliation. Facing the needs for healing in a congregation and in the lives of its members is also an act of seeking justice.

Application M-16E
Though not always easy, the singing of lament (a characteristic of many of the psalms) expresses a healthy honesty before God. Composers, congregations, and worship planners are encouraged to explore the use of songs of lament.

---

[55] Psalm 150:6.
[56] Alice Parker, *Melodious Accord* (Chicago: Liturgy Training Publications, 1991), 117-118.

Music serves God's mission

Principle M-17

The assembly is gathered and sent out in song, bearing the witness of Christ to each other and all they encounter. Through music, the Holy Spirit empowers the assembly to participate in God's mission to the world.

Background M-17A
The songs of the people are carried into and out of the assembly in a fluid and continuing process. "Worship is itself an aspect of the mission of God. . . . The liturgy sung, spoken, and *lived* is liturgy for a church in mission."[57]

Application M-17B
As the body of Christ, the assembly is by its very nature invitational. The church's music expresses that invitation. The gathering rite, the great thanksgiving, and the music at the communion all present opportunities to extend this invitational character of the liturgy.

Application M-17C
Witnessing to one another, the local community, and the world through the assembly's songs is a manifestation of the church's worship. With the congregation's song in their hearts and on their lips, people continue to proclaim the gospel in the world.

Application M-17D
Within the life of a congregation there are additional opportunities for music to contribute to the church's witness, such as concerts, pageants, oratorios, recitals, hymn festivals, revivals, evangelistic rallies, seeker services, and gatherings in the home.

---

57 Thomas H. Schattauer, "Liturgical Assembly Is Locus of Mission" in *Inside Out: Worship in an Age of Mission* (Minneapolis: Fortress Press, 1999), 5, 19.

Music proclaims justice and mercy

Principle M-18

Music bears the biblical word of justice and mercy.

Background M-18A
The biblical prophets called the people to do justice, love mercy, and walk humbly with God.[58] They also warned against worship that does not embody justice. "Take away from me the noise of your songs. . . . Let justice flow down like waters."[59]

Background M-18B
The prophetic witness of the church continues to call for justice and mercy today. "We realize the injustice and evil we face, but we sing and dance the gospel right into its midst."[60]

Background M-18C
Violence silences the violated. "Singing breaks the tyranny of this silence. It relates to the elemental human drive to sing" and beckons to justice and wholeness. Singing at worship gives voice to God's gift of sound where mercy and grace abound in word and sacrament for all people.[61]

Application M-18D
The assembly's call to act with justice and the call to praise God are woven together. Each presumes, stimulates, and supports the other. Music encourages hope, strengthening the singer and the assembly to do justice and love mercy.

Application M-18E
Christians recognize that there is much injustice in the world and yet maintain that God intends a just and orderly creation. In its ability to form community, music in worship enables us to more adequately address issues of justice and mercy in the world. In the midst of injustice and human brokenness, music in the assembly by God's grace can break open a space that helps us perceive God's design for a new creation.

[58] Micah 6:8.
[59] Amos 5:12, 23-24.
[60] Address by Pablo Sosa, Hymn Society Conference, University of British Columbia, Vancouver, Canada, July 13, 1999.
[61] Paul Westermeyer, *Let Justice Sing* (Collegeville: The Liturgical Press, 1998), 97.

Preaching

and the Christian Assembly

Part I: Proclamation and Preaching

God speaks

Principle P-1

God speaks. Within the Christian assembly gathered around word and sacrament, the triune God speaks to each person, to the community of faith, and to the whole creation.

Background P-1A
Before the preacher speaks a word, God has already spoken.[62] This same divine word is the word of promise proclaimed in the Christian assembly.

Background P-1B
Jesus Christ came to live among us and to speak our human words. In worship we hear the voice of Jesus calling us to repentance, announcing the good news to the poor, and inviting us to follow.

Background P-1C
The Holy Spirit calls and gathers the church around word and sacrament, so that all may be drawn to the living God. The Christian assembly is a sign to the whole world of God's presence.

[62] Genesis 1; John 1.

God's people proclaim the word

Principle P-2

God calls the whole people of God to proclaim the living word in worship, in witness, and in lives shaped by freedom in Christ.

Background P-2A

Within the assembly, proclamation of the word includes the public reading of the scripture, preaching, teaching, the celebration of the sacraments, confession and absolution, music, arts, prayers, Christian witness and service.[63]

Application P-2B

In worship, the people of God participate in proclamation through actively hearing and receiving the word. Those who lead in proclamation often find that their task is enriched when they provide intentional avenues for extending this participation, such as preparatory study of the scripture readings, call and response preaching, and sermon feedback groups.

Application P-2C

The shared responsibility for proclamation is demonstrated when, within worship, a number of people proclaim the word in various ways. In addition to those who preside and preach, there are those who read the scriptures, lead the prayers, encourage the assembly's song, and interpret the word through the arts.

Application P-2D

Through baptism God calls forth "a royal priesthood, a holy nation,"[64] that we may proclaim the praise of God and bear God's creative and redeeming word to all the world.[65] From the assembly, all the people are sent to lift up Jesus Christ in their daily lives.

---

[63] *The Use of the Means of Grace*, principles 6, 11, 12, application 5A (see appendix).
[64] Exodus 19:6; 1 Peter 2:9.
[65] Holy Baptism, *LBW*, 124.

Preaching is essential to the church

Principle P-3

In the assembly, preaching is a primary form of proclaiming the word of God. Preaching is, therefore, essential to the life of the church.

Background P-3A
Preaching has long held a place of importance among the many forms of proclamation in the assembly. In the synagogue, the rabbis and the elders not only read but also interpreted the scriptures, and Jesus himself read from the scroll and preached in his hometown of Nazareth (Luke 4). Justin, writing in the second century A.D., reports that, after the reading of the scriptures, "the presider exhorts and leads us into the pattern of these good things."[66] The sixteenth century reforming movements sought to restore the primacy and vitality of preaching. Still today, preaching is the "living and contemporary voice"[67] that links the witness of God's people throughout the ages with God's people in this time and place.

Application P-3B
Preaching is central to the assembly's proclamation. Preaching attends to the other aspects of proclamation, even as it speaks with its own distinct and lively voice.

Background P-3C
The Lutheran confessions identify preaching as one of the essential signs of the church. "The Christian church . . . is the assembly of all believers among whom the gospel is purely preached and the holy sacraments are administered according to that gospel."[68]

Background P-3D
People hunger for faithful preaching. Congregations consistently identify preaching among the highest priorities for ministry, worship, and leadership.[69]

---

[66] From The Apology of Justin Martyr (c. 150 A.D.) as quoted in *With One Voice*, 6.
[67] *The Use of the Means of Grace*, application 9A (see appendix).
[68] Augsburg Confession, Article VII, in *The Book of Concord: The Confessions of the Evangelical Lutheran Church*, ed. Robert Kolb and Timothy J. Wengert (Minneapolis: Fortress Press, 2000), 42.
[69] *The Future of Worship in the ELCA* (Chicago: Evangelical Lutheran Church in America, 1999), 72-75.

Preaching is part of the whole of worship

Principle P-4

Preaching in the assembly is integrated with the whole event of worship.

Application P-4A
The proclamation of the word and the celebration of the sacraments are intimately connected. Preaching unfolds the significance of baptism and leads to the eucharistic table; both preaching and the sacraments are empowered by the word of God's promise.[70]

Application P-4B
Preaching is attentive to other elements and influences of a given worship setting. Giving attention to the church year, songs, prayers, and events or emphases in the life of the congregation strengthens the ministry of preaching.

Application P-4C
Preaching is an integral part of celebrations of word and sacrament. In some liturgies, such as services of daily prayer, preaching may or may not be included. Other services specifically focused around the word, such as evangelistic services and revivals, may feature an expanded role for preaching and public teaching.

---

[70] *The Use of the Means of Grace,* principle 34 (see appendix).

Part II: Preaching and the Word of God

Preaching is spoken participation in the word

Principle P-5

The word of God is first of all a spoken word, an event that bears the power to create and to transform. Preaching participates in the creating and transforming power of God's word.

Background P-5A
The word *dabar* in Hebrew, the language of the Old Testament, is much like *logos* in Greek, the language of the New Testament. *Dabar* is at the same time both spoken word and action, both word and event. "By the word of the LORD the heavens were made, and all their host by the breath of his mouth. . . . For he spoke, and it came to be; he commanded, and it stood firm."[71]

Background P-5B
God formed a people through the word of promise and spoke words of judgment and hope to this people through the prophets. "My word . . . shall not return to me empty, but it shall accomplish that which I purpose, and succeed in the thing for which I sent it."[72]

Application P-5C
Preaching is primarily oral proclamation. Through human words, God continues to form people, speaking judgment and hope.

Application P-5D
All in the assembly are invited into the preaching event through the use of languages, signed or spoken, with which individual participants are most familiar. Providing translation or interpretation may be necessary to ensure communication.

---

[71] Psalm 33:6, 9.
[72] Isaiah 55:11.

Christ is present through preaching

Principle P-6

The word of God is embodied in the person of Jesus Christ, the Word of God incarnate. Jesus Christ is alive and present for us through preaching.

Background P-6A
"The Word became flesh, and lived among us . . . and we have seen his glory, glory as of a father's only son, full of grace and truth."[73]

Background P-6B
"For where Christ is not preached, there is no Holy Spirit to create, call, and gather the Christian church, apart from which no one can come to the Lord Christ."[74]

Application P-6C
Christian preaching consistently proclaims Jesus Christ crucified and risen. This preaching not only speaks the name of Jesus but also conveys the full measure of God's gifts to us in Christ.

---

[73] John 1:14.
[74] The Large Catechism, The Creed, The Third Article in *The Book of Concord*, 436.45.

Preaching is grounded in scripture

Principle P-7

The scriptures are the inspired witness to God's revealing acts in history. Preaching is grounded in these scriptures.

Background P-7A
"The canonical Scriptures of the Old and New Testaments are the written Word of God."[75]

Background P-7B
"Think of the scriptures as the loftiest and noblest of holy things, as the richest of mines which can never be sufficiently explored, in order that you may find that divine wisdom which God here lays before you in such simple guise as to quench all pride. Here you will find the swaddling cloths and the manger in which Christ lies."[76]

Background P-7C
"Preaching is the living and contemporary voice of one who interprets in all the Scriptures the things concerning Jesus Christ. In fidelity to the readings appointed for the day, the preacher proclaims our need of God's grace and freely offers that grace, equipping the community for mission and service in daily life."[77]

Background P-7D
A lectionary, a specific selection of biblical texts for the church year, is a valuable guide for preaching. The Revised Common Lectionary, widely used ecumenically, makes three lessons and a psalm available for each Sunday and festival, in a three-year cycle.

Application P-7E
Lectionary-based preaching connects the assembly with the wider church; guides the assembly through the church year; broadens preaching themes; and assists in preparatory study of the scripture texts by preachers and assembly members. There may be occasions when the preacher employs scriptural texts other than lectionary readings.

---

[75] *Constitution, Bylaws, and Continuing Resolutions of the Evangelical Lutheran Church in America*, 1995, 2.02.
[76] "Prefaces to the Old Testament," in *Luther's Works*, Volume 35 (Philadelphia: Fortress Press, 1960), 236.
[77] *The Use of the Means of Grace*, application 9A (see appendix).

Application P-7F

Preaching is one way in which the people of God encounter scripture, and by which lives of faith are formed and reformed. This encounter necessitates the preacher's own entry into the texts, while studying and grappling with them. The preaching event is deepened when the people of God also live with the biblical story in prayer, study, and devotional reading.

Application P-7G

Preaching will in part tell the biblical story so that those who do not know it may hear. Preaching will also proclaim the biblical story so that all may be formed in faith.

The word of God is both law and gospel

Principle P-8

The proclamation of God's word is both law and gospel. Preaching makes a careful and pastoral distinction between these two aspects of the word of God.

Background P-8A
The law of God is first a gift from God, God's gracious pattern for creation and for human relationships that offers life and peace in community.[78] Martin Luther drew upon the insights of the apostle Paul to identify another use of the law. The law convicts people of sin and at the same time reflects the broken nature of human existence. Thus the law drives us to look for help from someone who can deliver us from the depths of our human predicament.[79]

Background P-8B
The gospel is God's promise of forgiveness and gracious reconciliation. God loves us and all creation with an everlasting love. We are reconciled to God through Jesus Christ, crucified and risen. The Holy Spirit continues to form our lives with gifts of grace and to empower us in bearing witness to the good news.

Application P-8C
The preaching of the law brings a word of judgment to our estrangement from God and diagnoses the depth of human need. The preaching of the gospel conveys to us God's forgiveness and new life with a word of hope that answers our deepest need.

Application P-8D
This distinction between law and gospel is a central key to interpreting the scriptures, rather than a pattern for sermon design. Law and gospel describes how the word is received through the power of the Spirit.

---

[78] Romans 2:12.
[79] Galatians 3:23, 24.

The Spirit calls people to faith

Principle P-9

The Holy Spirit calls people to faith through preaching.

Background P-9A
"Faith comes from what is heard, and what is heard comes through the word of Christ."[80]

Background P-9B
According to the Small Catechism, the Spirit calls us through the gospel, enlightens us with gifts of the Spirit, makes us holy, and keeps us in the true faith.[81] The Spirit is at work in the ministry of preaching.

Application P-9C
Preaching witnesses to the saving grace of Jesus Christ, inviting the assembly into new and renewed relationship with the living God. This invitation is extended both to longtime Christians and those new to the assembly. The church is renewed when preaching is ever more outgoing, invitational, welcoming, and intentionally accessible to those with little church background or familiarity with scripture, even as preaching leads the entire assembly toward maturity of faith.

Application P-9D
Preaching frees and empowers the people of God to continue their witness beyond the assembly, enabling us to share the good news of Jesus Christ with others.

---

[80] Romans 10:17.
[81] The Small Catechism, The Creed, The Third Article, in *The Book of Concord,* 355.

Preaching shapes people's lives

Principle P-10

The Holy Spirit works through preaching, forming and empowering people to carry out the mission of God in their daily lives.

Application P-10A
Preaching calls all the baptized to die and to rise anew with Christ each day, so that they might carry out their ministries in the power of the resurrection.

Application P-10B
Preaching speaks God's word into our daily lives.[82] Through preaching the Holy Spirit renews and empowers us to serve God in all that we do: at home, in relationships, through work, in public life, and in the church.

Application P-10C
Preaching speaks honestly and openly to difficult issues and choices. Preaching exhorts people to seek the Holy Spirit's guidance in discerning faithful decisions and actions.

Application P-10D
Scripture ties the living of each day to God's call to justice. God's prophetic word is not neutral when dealing with the hurts and pains of the oppressed and voiceless. Preaching confronts issues such as racism, prejudice, discrimination, and internalized oppression[83] with the liberating word of God.

Application P-10E
Core Christian teachings can be enlisted in preaching God's mercy and justice. God's justifying grace summons preachers to proclaim justice. God's will for justice is good news to those who are poor, captive, oppressed, and all who are on the margins of society.

---

[82] "Affirmation of the Vocation of Christians in the World" in *Occasional Services: A Companion to Lutheran Book of Worship* (Minneapolis: Augsburg Fortress, 1982), 147 and "Affirmation of the Vocation of the Baptized in the World" in *Welcome to Christ: Lutheran Rites for the Catechumenate* (Minneapolis, Augsburg Fortress, 1997), 58.
[83] Ivis LaRiviere-Mestre, *Field Work Manual: A Cultural Awareness Resource* (unpublished), 32.

Part III: The Ministry of Preaching

God authorizes preaching

Principle P-11

God authorizes the ministry of preaching.

Background P-11A

The authority of preaching is, in part, an extension of Jesus' own mission of preaching the reign of God.[84] The authority of preaching is a servant authority, rooted in the mercy of God and is bestowed by the one who "humbled himself, taking the form of a servant."[85]

Application P-11B

In a world of conflicting voices of authority, in a time that questions any ultimate authority, we are bold to claim ultimate authority for preaching. This authority is a gift of God, the author of creation, rather than being based on any human prerogative, institutional claim, or appeal to certitude. We are authorized by God to tell the story of God's revealing work as witnessed to by the scriptures. We believe that the telling of this story has the power to inspire and convince people of its life-giving power.

Application P-11C

Those who preach are persuaded that the promises of God can be trusted, and they preach in that confidence. Through the word preached in the assembly, the community of faith comes to know this word of God to be trustworthy, and thus authoritative in their lives.

---

[84] Matthew 28:28, Luke 10:16.
[85] Philippians 2:11.

The church calls and equips preachers

Principle P-12

The church entrusts specific people with the ministry of preaching and equips them for continuing growth in this responsibility.

Background P-12A
"Called and ordained ministers bear responsibility for the preached Word in the Church gathered for public worship."[86] "While other persons sometimes preach, the called pastor of a congregation has responsibility for this preaching, ordinarily preparing and delivering the sermon and overseeing all public ministry of the word in the congregation."[87] In our congregations, the pastor charged with oversight for preaching, a congregational council, or a bishop may authorize lay persons to preach.

Application P-12B
The church calls those who preach to the work of careful preparation. This preparation includes humility before God's word, an immersion in the scriptures, diligent study of the texts, and the use of tools of interpretation that support the preaching task. Preaching in Lutheran settings also calls for familiarity with and faithfulness to the Lutheran confessions and ecumenical creeds.

Application P-12C
When those who preach prepare with others, preaching is enriched. Listening to the people given to the preacher's care, studying the word with those who will hear it, exploring the texts with other preachers—all these strengthen the ministry of preaching.

Application P-12D
Providing resources, training, and continuing education that assist in the formation of those who preach is a fundamental responsibility of this church. Preachers look to the church for support in study, renewal, and growth in biblical and theological understanding, as well as training in communication forms and skills.

---

[86] *The Use of the Means of Grace*, principle 9 (see appendix).
[87] *The Use of the Means of Grace*, application 9B (see appendix).

Life in community nourishes preaching

Principle P-13

Life in the Christian community is a gift that forms and nourishes the ministry of preaching.

Application P-13A
Preaching that declares God's love to all in need is strengthened when those who preach grapple first with their own need of God's healing. Along with all of God's people, the preacher is addressed, exposed, and beloved by God.

Application P-13B
The formation of preachers involves integration of the living word into their lives, both in preparatory training and as a lifelong practice. A variety of spiritual disciplines, such as prayer, devotional reading, sabbath keeping, hospitality, and service, can assist in this formation.

Application P-13C
Those who preach are formed by the communities in which they serve. They stand in the midst of the people in joy and in sorrow, receiving as well as giving comfort and admonition. They are strengthened in knowing that they do not have all the words, nor could they, but that they serve in partnership with Christ and the whole people of God.

Part IV: Preaching in Context

Preaching is contextual

Principle P-14

God, who spoke at creation, through the incarnate Word, through the prophets and apostles, continues to speak into our times and places. Preaching connects the one holy catholic and apostolic witness with the many particular and overlapping contexts of our day.

Background P-14A
"Contextualization is a necessary task for the Church's mission in the world, so that the Gospel can be ever more deeply rooted in diverse local cultures."[88]

Background P-14B
Communities are characterized by overlapping particularities, including ethnic, historic, socioeconomic, ecclesiastical, and generational factors, among others. Within those communities, people come to worship with a variety of theological perspectives, different degrees of familiarity with the biblical story, and varying expectations of preaching. All of these stories and perspectives influence the way in which the word of life is proclaimed and heard.

Application P-14C
We invite and expect all members of the assembly, including children, to listen to, respond to, and share in the proclamation of the word in all its forms. Those who preach respect all members of the assembly, especially children, by preaching the word clearly and not manipulating or trivializing any individual or group.

Application P-14D
Those who preach are attentive to the congregation, the particular occasion, the local community in all its diversity, and the global context, so that the word may be shaped in ways that reinforce its meaning and power in each situation.

---

[88] "Nairobi Statement on Worship and Culture" in *Christian Worship: Unity in Cultural Diversity*, ed. S. Anita Stauffer (Geneva: Lutheran World Federation, 1996), 3.1. See the introduction to this volume, pp. viii-x, for a fuller summary of this document.

Application P-14E

Those who preach bring their daily encounters with the people among whom they serve into dialogue with their encounters with scripture and the church's tradition. An urgent willingness to be with people in their various circumstances—their burdens and dilemmas, joys and fulfillments—nourishes preaching that speaks to people's lives. At the same time, those who preach are careful to safeguard people's confidences.

Background P-14F

Our context is increasingly a mission field, where the story of God's people and Christian images of salvation coexist with images and stories from popular culture, current affairs, and other religious traditions. These images powerfully shape the minds and spirits of contemporary people.

Application P-14G

Those who preach are challenged to find the connections and define the differences between God's story and other stories alive in the culture, seeking the signs of God's reign at work in the world beyond the assembly.

Application P-14H

The context of a community includes particular events beyond weekly worship gatherings. God's word is also proclaimed in worship when people gather to celebrate a marriage, to bury their dead, and for other special occasions. These gathered communities influence the way the word is proclaimed, without altering the essential life-giving message of Jesus Christ.[89]

---

[89] *The Use of the Means of Grace,* principle 13 (see appendix).

Preaching is countercultural

Principle P-15

At times the word of God contradicts the prevailing assumptions of a particular culture or time. Preaching the word of God is often countercultural.

Background P-15A

"Some components of every culture in the world are sinful, dehumanizing, and contradictory to the values of the Gospel. From the perspective of the Gospel, they need critique and transformation. Contextualization of Christian faith and worship necessarily involves challenging of all types of oppression and social injustice wherever they exist in earthly cultures."[90]

Application P-15B

The preaching of the law is often more realistic and honest about the depths of human need and the brokenness of our world, when compared with common cultural understandings. Likewise, the preaching of the gospel is often far more genuinely hopeful and life-giving.

---

[90] Nairobi Statement, 4.1.

Preaching is transcultural and cross-cultural

Principle P-16

God's word unites people across cultures in faith, hope, and love.

Background P-16A
Preaching is transcultural. "The resurrected Christ whom we worship, and through whom by the power of the Holy Spirit we know the grace of the Triune God, transcends and indeed is beyond all cultures." [91]

Background P-16B
Preaching is cross-cultural. "Jesus came to be the Savior of all people. He welcomes the treasures of earthly cultures into the city of God."[92]

Application P-16C
Preaching takes on a cross-cultural character when images, insights, and preaching practices from one locality of the church are borrowed for use in another locality. In this way, the local assembly consciously participates in the expressions of the wider church. The use of biblical texts from other times and places is itself an example of this cross-cultural sharing.

Application P-16D
The incarnation means God's grace is manifest in our many cultural expressions and necessarily finds voice in the preached word of God both in form and substance. Insights and practices regarding preaching that come from a variety of cultures enrich the whole church. We welcome and seek to learn from other models of preaching that are gifts from the breadth of the Christian tradition.

Application P-16E
The expressions of faith from other cultures can fruitfully turn the attention of preacher and assembly alike to their own preconceptions and limitations and thereby open the gospel for them in a new way. We are called not only to know the stories of our neighbors throughout the world, but to walk with each other in our joys and trials.

[91] Nairobi Statement, 2.1.
[92] Nairobi Statement, 5.1.

Preaching relies on various tools of communication

Principle P-17

Preaching uses the tools of human communication to convey the message of divine grace. The craft of preaching involves continually developing these tools, for the sake of communicating God's word.

Background P-17A
In word and sacrament the Holy Spirit works through earthly things—bread, wine, water, word—to bring the infinite God into the physical and spiritual wholeness of each person. The word is carried by finite means such as words spoken and sung, print, visual images, bodies, signs, and gestures.

Application P-17B
Preaching in the assembly is a live interaction between preacher and all who are gathered. Preachers use a variety of means to communicate the gospel. Tools and techniques employed by preachers are always servants of the gospel rather than ends in themselves.

Application P-17C
Preaching relies primarily on tools of oral communication. Those who preach give attention to such matters as choice of language, structure, coherence, imagery, tone, rhythm, meter and pace; dialects, idioms, concepts, and metaphors from contemporary experience; the appropriate use of humor, story, illustration, gesture, and emotion.

Application P-17D
Some congregations include special sermons for children in the assembly. Our churches hold varying points of view about the value of such sermons. When this form of preaching occurs, the same care, respect, attention to communication, adequate preparation, and concern for the gospel are needed as in all preaching. Sharing the word with children is integrated into the whole of worship.

Application P-17E
Modes of communication change as human cultures change. Developments in technology and media influence not only what, but how, people communicate and understand. Numerous modes of communication, such as art, visual design, drama, film, and projected presentation may be able to support the preaching of the word. Preachers will prayerfully examine and use these means with care, even as they are careful in choosing language and tone for proclamation.

Worship Space

and the Christian Assembly

Part I: Worship, Worship Space, and Mission

Worship is spatial

Principle S-1

Worship and worship space are linked in a vital relationship.

Background S-1A

The first Christians spoke of their communal shelter and worship space as the "house of the church" (*domus ecclesiae*). Family dwellings became venues for worship not only because of persecutions but also because of theological convictions. Early Christian tradition spoke of the gathered assembly in relation to its place: "It is not a place that is called 'church,' nor a house made of stones and earth. . . . What then is the church? It is the holy assembly of those who live in righteousness."[93] Over the centuries, the building itself became identified as *church,* yet the assembly remains the primary expression of the church.

Application S-1B

A worshiping community is renewed by an informed examination of the patterns and actions of liturgy, the naming of that assembly's expression of the liturgy, and an understanding of the relationship of worship to the arts that participate in it. This journey of discovery can assist the community in the imaginative use of an existing space, the renovation of a current space, or the construction of a new space for worship.

---

[93] *The Apostolic Tradition of Hippolytus,* trans. Burton Scott Easton (Ann Arbor: Cambridge University Press, 1939).

Space expresses faith and serves mission

Principle S-2

The place of worship expresses the church's faith and serves God's mission.

Background S-2A
The scriptures, the Lutheran confessions, churchwide statements such as *The Use of the Means of Grace,* and resources from other churches serve in varying ways as guidelines for the evaluation of existing or new spaces for worship.

Application S-2B
The primary criteria for ordering worship spaces are sound worship practices. Local patterns of worship are weighed in the light of ecumenical and churchwide principles.

Application S-2C
Cultural faith expressions are at the heart of particular communities. God's mission is served when attention is given to an assembly's cultural expressions of faith and when worship space accommodates a variety of such expressions.

Application S-2D
Many rooms for worship are configured and appointed in ways that inhibit the worship of the assembly. Renewed understandings of worship may call for creative use of existing space or the reordering of worship space so that it better serves the church's worship and mission.

Application S-2E
Worship forms people for Christian ministry. The space and its visual appointments share in the formation of those called to be Christ's body in the world, proclaiming the word through nonverbal means, teaching the faith through image and symbol, and offering their own witness to the gospel. Christian mission is enlivened by and inseparable from the worship of the assembly.

Various spaces serve a common pattern of worship

Principle S-3

Spaces used for worship vary from place to place and from culture to culture, accommodating a common liturgical pattern.

Background S-3A
Many churches today are reaffirming a basic liturgical pattern for the primary weekly assembly that was shaped in the early centuries of the church and renewed during the Reformation era.

> Sunday is the primary day on which the Church assembles: the first day of creation when God transformed darkness into light and the day on which Christ rose from death and revealed himself to the disciples in the scriptures and the breaking of bread. The baptized gather to hear the word, to pray for those in need, to offer thanks to God for the gift of salvation, to receive the bread of life and the cup of blessing, and to be renewed for the daily witness of faith, hope, and love.[94]

Background S-3B
A recent study on worship and culture suggests that worship relates dynamically to culture in four ways. It is *transcultural*, the same substance for everyone everywhere, beyond culture. It is *contextual*, varying according to the local situation (both natural and cultural). It is *countercultural*, challenging what is contrary to the gospel in a given culture. Finally, it is *cross-cultural*, making possible sharing between different local cultures.[95]

Application S-3C
Because the Spirit has spoken and continues to speak to Christian assemblies in all times and places, worship spaces are planned and created to express common norms within the local culture and community. Affirmation of locality is balanced, however, by countercultural commitments to justice, stewardship, and the integrity of design, materials, and appointments. Embracing artistic and architectural styles from a variety of cultures enriches worship and encourages a broader experience of the church catholic.

---

[94] *With One Voice*, 8.
[95] "Nairobi Statement on Worship and Culture," in *Christian Worship: Unity in Cultural Diversity*, ed. S. Anita Stauffer (Geneva: Lutheran World Federation, 1996), 1.3. See the introduction to this volume, pp. viii-x, for a fuller summary of this document.

Sacred worship creates sacred space

Principle S-4

The body of Christ gathered in prayer hallows the space used for worship.

Background S-4A

The scriptures speak of the people of God as "living stones . . . built into a spiritual house."[96] Gathered to Christ, the cornerstone precious in God's sight, the worshiping assembly is a place where God makes a home. Christ's presence is promised not under certain architectural forms but where two or three are gathered in his name.[97]

Background S-4B

For the first three centuries, Christians generally rejected the religious architecture of the day. They did not accept the dividing line between sacred and secular; the whole world was a place to encounter God. Rather than otherworldly places for worship they found the presence of God expressed in the awesome "this world-ness" of Christ's presence.

Background S-4C

From ancient days, the dedication of a worship space was accomplished by the first eucharistic celebration of the community. The common worship of the community created an uncommon place to experience the mystery of God's presence.

Application S-4D

The worship of the assembly, rather than architectural or artistic expression, creates sacred space. Architecture, furnishings, works of art, liturgical vessels, and other elements of the rites reach their noblest aim when they facilitate the sacred celebration of the people gathered for worship.

Application S-4E

The sacred touches people in the ordinary. God is present throughout creation. Effective use of natural light, flowing water, plants, and other natural materials contributes to our experience of the sacred.

---

[96] 1 Peter 2:5.
[97] Matthew 18:20.

The arts serve the worshiping assembly

Principle S-5

Art and architecture proclaim the gospel, enrich the assembly's participation in the word and sacraments, and reinforce the themes of the occasion and season. Liturgical art animates the life and faith of the community.

Background S-5A
"Music, the visual arts, and the environment of our worship spaces embody the proclamation of the Word. . . ."[98] "The visual arts and the spaces for worship assist the congregation to participate in worship, to focus on the essentials, and to embody the Gospel."[99]

Application S-5B
When an art form participates in the liturgical action, it becomes an instrument of proclamation rather than decoration or ornamentation. Liturgical art reinforces and articulates the themes of the liturgy. Through rhythm, sound, smell, form, texture, color, and light, liturgical art is a powerful language that speaks to all the human senses.

Background S-5C
The Spirit of Christ has spoken and continues to speak through a variety of voices: individual and communal, past and present. Worship spaces use architectural styles evocative of specific times and cultures. Architecture as a living art explores new forms of expression, construction techniques, and building materials. Form and style constantly change as architecture seeks more effective ways to facilitate a faith community's worship needs.

Application S-5D
Sensitive and appropriate use of ethnic or cultural artistic forms that are not indigenous to the setting in which they are employed can open avenues of communion and ministry.

Application S-5E
The balance between everchanging styles and enduring values is an ongoing challenge for planners of the house of the church. This creative tension calls for deliberate efforts to express the timeless in a timely fashion.

---

[98] *The Use of the Means of Grace*, principle 11 (see appendix).
[99] *The Use of the Means of Grace*, application 11B (see appendix).

Application S-5F

Some expressions of art, addressing themes related to the whole of Christian liturgy, may be permanent or infrequently changing. Other artistic expressions have temporary application to occasional rites or specific seasons of the liturgical year. The preparation of a space to celebrate the seasons of the church year begins with the study of liturgical texts and readings. Artists, amateur and professional, are encouraged to collaborate with worship leaders and seasonal planning teams so that their work is focused on the assembly and its worship.

Worship space witnesses to justice

Principle S-6

Worship space witnesses to the gospel in ways that challenge destructive patterns within society and affirm justice, peace, and the integrity of God's creation.

Application S-6A

The concern for social justice and the building of beautiful structures need not be opposing values. All human beings long for an experience of beauty that leads to worship. The creation of a beautiful place need not be determined by how much it costs. A community with limited resources may have a greater need for a beautiful worship space than a congregation of substantial economic means. Beauty can be expressed with quality materials that are used with integrity and are appropriate to a given space.

Application S-6B

Decisions relating to architecture, design, construction materials, and ongoing maintenance can be made with environmental sensitivity and a foundation of good stewardship.

Application S-6C

The way a building relates to an environment or neighborhood is a sign of a community's attitude. Buildings can be welcoming or foreboding, inviting or imposing. A worship space that welcomes and accommodates other activities such as concerts, lectures, and dramas reveals a stewardship of resources and commitment to the greater community.

Application S-6D

One common meaning of the term sanctuary is a place of protection and refuge. A liturgical space may serve a congregation and the larger community as a place of safety and refreshment, accessible for prayer and meditation, at times other than when the whole assembly gathers.

Application S-6E

Worship space that reflects intentional consideration of the diversity of culture and ethnic background within the congregation and its surrounding community is one way of expressing a commitment to social justice.

Part II: Areas of Liturgical Action

There are liturgical centers within the worship space

Principle S-7

The assembly space includes primary centers for the celebration of the word of God and the sacraments, secondary areas that facilitate the roles of all the leaders, and other spaces that complement the requirements of communal worship.

Background S-7A
The foundational symbol of the church is the gathered assembly itself, which transcends every barrier, such as class, ethnicity, and age. In the New Testament, the Greek term *synerchomai* (*gather* or *come together*) expresses this distinctive character of Christian worship.[100] The Augsburg Confession declares, "The church is the assembly of saints in which the gospel is taught purely and the sacraments are administered rightly."[101] There is broad ecumenical agreement that the assembly is the starting place in the task of understanding and renewing worship and the place of worship.

Application S-7B
The unity of the entire worship room proclaims the unity of the assembly, gathered into one in Christ. Communicating a sense of oneness and wholeness as a gathering place of the baptized community is of first importance, followed by consideration of different areas within the space that correspond to different roles and functions in the liturgy.

Background S-7C
Just as a home has areas for bathing, sleeping, eating, and refreshment, so the assembly organizes its worship life around liturgical places of gathering and sending, baptizing, reading and preaching, celebrating the Lord's supper, and ritual interaction among the assembled people. Each area has its own special character and each is a sign of the presence of Christ.

---

[100] 1 Corinthians 11:17-34.
[101] Augsburg Confession, Article VII, in *The Book of Concord: The Confessions of the Evangelical Lutheran Church,* ed. Robert Kolb and Timothy J. Wengert (Minneapolis: Fortress Press, 2000), 43.

Background S-7D

An order for the Dedication of a Church Building[102] suggests a procession from threshold doors to font, pulpit, altar-table, and then into the midst of the people, thus identifying the focal points of a worship space. At each place a blessing is said, and ritual acts including touching water in the font, placing a Bible or lectionary, and vesting the altar may accompany this liturgy.

Application S-7E

Each piece of liturgical furniture and area of liturgical action has its own character and requirements. Worship is enhanced when all furnishings taken together possess a unity and harmony with each other and with the architecture of the room and when the craft and imagination of the artist are reflected in the quality of these furnishings.

---

[102] *Occasional Services,* 166-171.

The place of baptism proclaims our faith

Principle S-8

The place and the practices of baptism proclaim the church's faith. A generous space around flowing water reinforces the meaning of baptism for the assembly.

Background S-8A

Although baptism has always been central in Lutheran theology, in practice it has not always been accorded a central place in liturgy or liturgical spaces. Often fonts are small and placed in remote locations. A contribution of the ecumenical liturgical movement has been to emphasize Holy Baptism as a consequential sign of faith for adults and children.

Application S-8B

Access to the font affirms the communal nature of baptism. When the place of baptism is near the main entrance, the understanding of baptism as the sacrament of Christian birth and as commissioning for ministry is reinforced. Wherever the font is located, it serves its role best when it is visible and there is sufficient space for gathering around it. At times, children in the assembly may be invited to gather closest to the baptismal group.

Application S-8C

The most critical sign of baptism is the water itself. The rich biblical understanding of baptism as bath,[103] as new birth,[104] and as burial and resurrection with Christ[105] is best expressed when abundant water is used. Where a font large enough to permit adults and children to enter the water is unavailable, one large enough to allow pouring with abundant water is an alternative. Non-porous flooring beneath and surrounding the font accommodates the generous use of water at baptism.

Application S-8D

Keeping the font filled with fresh or flowing water at all times, and not only when baptisms are scheduled, enables the faithful continually to affirm their baptism by sight, sound, and touch. A permanent baptismal place may enable the continuous flow of fresh water to the font.

---

[103] 1 Corinthians 6:11.
[104] John 3:5.
[105] Romans 6:3-5.

Application S-8E

Usually located near the font, a paschal candle is a preeminent symbol of the light of Christ, used to proclaim the crucified and risen Christ especially during the Easter season and at baptisms and funerals.

Background S-8F

In scripture and Christian tradition, anointing with oil has been an important sign in rites of baptism, healing, and times of passage. In the rite of baptism, oil has been used in association with the laying of hands as a sign of the gift of the Holy Spirit and of sealing the faith.

Application S-8G

The growing appreciation of the use of oil in rites of baptism and healing suggests the usefulness of a place in close proximity to the baptismal font where anointing oil may be kept and possibly displayed to view.

There is a focal point for the word

Principle S-9

Placing a Bible or lectionary on an ambo or pulpit brings to visible expression the presence and importance of the word of God.

Background S-9A

"The use of a Bible or lectionary of appropriate size and dignity by those who read the Scriptures aloud, the use of this book in liturgical processions, and its placement on the reading desk or pulpit may bring the centrality of the Word to visible expression."[106]

Application S-9B

Whether called the ambo, reading desk, or pulpit, the place of the word best fulfills its role when it is dignified and human-sized. It visually expresses the authority of the word of God without overly elevating the reader or preacher or separating them from the congregation. Proclamation is aided when everyone in the congregation can see and hear those who stand at the ambo and when its size and design are proportionate within the worship space as a whole.

Application S-9C

The distinction between the place of reading (lectern) and place of preaching (pulpit) may suggest an artificial hierarchy of ministries and of scripture readings. Although reading and preaching occasionally occur in other locations within the assembly, the proclamation of the word of God is honored by the creation of a single focal point.[107]

---

[106] *The Use of the Means of Grace,* application 7B (see appendix).
[107] *The Use of the Means of Grace,* principles 7 and 9 (see appendix).

The table of Christ is set

Principle S-10

The table of our Lord Jesus Christ is set in the midst of the assembly.

Background S-10A
Before and after his passion, Jesus shared meals with disciples and others as a sign of the kingdom. The eucharistic altar has taken many shapes throughout Christian history. Designs that suggest a table for dining have been used to reinforce the nature of the eucharist as meal.

Application S-10B
The altar is the holy table of the Christian family. Carefully crafted of worthy, solid material, its size and shape are proportionate to the size and shape of the worship space. The mensa or top of the table accommodates the bread and wine of the eucharist and those who minister around it. The table itself is the primary symbol, making secondary symbolism unnecessary. The altar can be vested with a white cloth (fair linen) and paraments that complement its shape.

Application S-10C
The meal is prepared and the table is set for the baptized people of God. The goals of easy access and a sense of gathering around the table suggest a careful reexamination of the place and use of altar rails.

Application S-10D
The altar is the common table of the assembly. It has a central role in the liturgy but need not be spatially centered. Because the altar-table is not the only liturgical focus of the room but parallels other centers in importance, an offcenter arrangement may be suitable in some contexts.

Worship leaders have a place

Principle S-11

The worship space includes designated spaces for worship leaders. The place for presiding and assisting ministers is distinct, but not overly separated or elevated.

Background S-11A

A significant liturgical space in synagogue worship is the place of elders who are responsible for presiding at the worship service. When Jesus preached at the synagogue in Nazareth, after reading from the Isaiah scroll, "he rolled up the scroll and gave it back to the attendant and sat down."[108] From the chair of the leader, he then preached his brief but powerful sermon.

Background S-11B

The concept of a presider's chair for the bishop *(cathedra)* developed from one use of the Roman civil basilica, in which the chair was the place for the judge or representative of the royalty. The presider was seated in the chair, which was located in the center of the apse and surrounded by other benches for the bishop's presbyters, and the assembly stood. A similar practice is still retained in some civic courtrooms, where the judge is seated as people stand.

Background S-11C

Many churches, especially in various Protestant traditions, reflect a wide variety of approaches and some ambivalence in the matter of seating liturgical leaders. The idea of an ecclesiastical throne is questioned. At the other end of the spectrum, in some places the commonality of people and ministers is expressed by having leaders sit among the people.

Application S-11D

Even though there is reason to stress the oneness of the assembly and its leaders, the roles and functions of leaders call for designated places for leaders that are somewhat separate and clearly visible.

---

[108] Luke 4:20-21.

Musical leaders have a place

Principle S-12

Providing adequate areas for choirs and instrumentalists allows them to function effectively as worship leaders.

Background S-12A
Musical leaders and musical groups often need to be shaped into ensembles. The organ, piano, and other accompanying instruments typically need to be close to choirs, cantors, and other musical leaders.

Application S-12B
Places designated for instruments and musical leaders facilitate their roles in animating the assembly's worship without overshadowing the visual centers of word and sacrament or impeding the ritual action of the assembly. When the place for leading music resembles a stage, musicians may be perceived primarily as performers. Judicious placement of voices and instruments helps to ensure that the making of music is an offering within the liturgy.

Application S-12C
When musical leaders have an integral place within the main assembly space, rather than being separated in a balcony or transept, the sense of the unity of the assembly may be heightened and congregational song strengthened. Planners should consider configurations that enable musical leaders to be seen and heard without obscuring the primary symbols of ambo, table, and font. Flexible seating and flat floors are conducive to various spatial arrangements.

Application S-12D
Acoustics for worship are designed primarily to encourage the common voice of the assembly. Sound needs to mix and move in the assembly. Lively acoustical spaces are most often fostered by hard, reflective surfaces and a limited use of carpeting or other absorbent material.

The gathering place welcomes and sends forth

Principle S-13

The gathering place (commons or narthex) is a significant transitional space between church and world. The gathering space builds a sense of community, facilitates hospitality, and sends forth the assembly into the world. It may also serve as a starting place for processions.

Application S-13A

The physical environment outside the place of worship contributes to gathering and preparing the community for worship. Intentionally configured parking areas, entries, and exits, as well as areas set apart for seating and conversation, welcome newcomers and provide a hospitable path for the whole assembly from and to the world. Landscaping, gardens, and surrounding areas are part of the structure and of the community's welcome to worship.

Application S-13B

A generous and functional gathering place (sometimes called the commons or narthex) facilitates welcome and hospitality. The gathering place provides opportunity both to strengthen the congregation's own sense of community and to invite visitors into the assembly. Ample and inviting doorways mark the transition from gathering space to worship space and accommodate various rites and movements.

Application S-13C

The purpose of the commons area is enhanced when kitchen facilities, coatrooms, washrooms, nursery, and other ancillary spaces offer easy access and consistent design. A vesting sacristy located near the gathering area allows ministers to greet arriving people and to assemble for processions.

Application S-13D

When the gathering space is generous in scale and well-appointed, it serves as an effective area for hospitality and community-building beyond its uses before and after worship. Such a space is often conducive to other educational, liturgical, and social activities.

Many rites shape worship spaces

Principle S-14

The entire ritual life of the congregation contributes to the shape of worship spaces.

Application S-14A
The recovery of the fullness of Holy Baptism has resulted in the recovery of the powerful liturgies of Holy Week and the Three Days (Triduum). The planning of worship spaces takes into account the spatial requirements for celebrating these liturgies. Dramatic readings, stational liturgies, the stripping of the altar, foot washing, veneration of the cross, lighting of the new fire, and the lavish rites of baptism and eucharist call for generous and appropriate places for congregational participation.

Background S-14B
Worship spaces also provide for the celebration of non-eucharistic rites and occasions, which may include services of the word, rites of passage such as marriage and burial, daily prayer, evangelistic events, and liturgical dramas.

Application S-14C
The witness of God's love in liturgies relating to death and burial is communicated in a worship space where the assuring signs of baptism are strongly present in the use of pall, paschal candle, placement of coffin or urn, and procession. Cemeteries and columbaria are liturgical venues that may need to accommodate family and community gatherings.

Application S-14D
The growing practice of cremation invites the local congregation to provide a columbarium as a service to the congregation and a spatial witness to the continued union with the church triumphant. A columbarium provides niches for cremated remains in an attendant space such as a chapel or a memorial garden.

---

[109] *The Use of the Means of Grace,* principles 47 and 48 (see appendix).

Background S-14E

"The bread and wine of communion are handled with care and reverence, out of a sense of the value both of what has been set apart by the Word as a bearer of Christ and of God's good creation. . . . Congregations provide for communion of the sick, homebound, and imprisoned."[109]

Application S-14F

Congregations that provide communion for those who are absent may need a worthy cabinet (ambry) for temporary storage of the elements, located in the sacristy or another suitable place.

Media serves liturgy

Principle S-15

The use of electronic media and technology in a worship space presents both opportunities and challenges for the church's worship.

Application S-15A

The use of audiovisual elements in worship requires careful consideration. Such media are desirable when they enhance rather than replace essential congregational action. Their function of assisting the assembly's participation in worship through the visual arts may include providing the color and form of seasonal artwork. Because of the many ramifications of the use of this technology in worship, careful integration must be assured. Technological equipment (sound boards, light systems, microphones, speakers, cameras, projectors, video screens) is most effective when it does not impair liturgical movement, obscure primary symbols (meal, preaching, baptism), or adversely affect the design of the space and its worship. Sound reinforcement, when necessary, is held in careful balance with natural acoustics. The effective use of media and technology often calls for particular skills and training.

Application S-15B

Media and technology can also assist in overcoming physical limitations, aid sight for the visually impaired, and augment sound for the hearing impaired, facilitating everyone's full participation.

Cross, clothing, and vessels contribute to proclamation

Principle S-16

The visual arts and forms of media embody and support the proclamation of the word of God.

Application S-16A

Although a wall-mounted or hanging cross is a familiar feature of many worship spaces, the assembly can be brought to a deeper realization of the power of this saving sign when the cross is carried in procession and placed in the midst of the people. The impact of this action is enhanced by a processional cross of strong and simple design that is the primary cross in the worship space.

Application S-16B

In the creation of vestments and paraments, color, texture, and design predominate over intricate patterns. Vestments celebrate the community's worship and the ministry of its leaders. Graceful full-length albs, as a sign of baptism, are appropriate for all worship leaders, including the choir. In some congregations, during the Easter season, the newly baptized are clothed in albs.

Background S-16C

Throughout history, the church has made use of the visual arts. From early Christian paintings in underground catacombs to the stained glass of medieval cathedrals, the visual arts have been used to aid participation in worship and proclamation of the gospel.

Application S-16D

Art that is permanent and seasonal is evaluated according to its artistic quality and liturgical effectiveness. Art that draws attention to itself as an independent element tends to distract from the community's worship. Artwork created by children and communal artistic efforts are used effectively when integrated into a plan that reinforces the liturgy and the worship space.

Background S-16E

Crosses, icons, and other symbols have been visual signs of Christian identity and faith. Their use has occasioned significant debate and division throughout history. Some Christian traditions have continued using symbols inherited through the ages. Other churches have moved in the direction of spaces devoid of traditional symbols. The church continues to assess the use of symbols in liturgical spaces to discern their meaning theologically, pastorally, and aesthetically.

Application S-16F

When Christians identify symbols that organize their common worship life, the most important visual elements in a worship space are the assembly itself, bread and wine, water, and the book of the scriptures. The cross is central to our understanding of the faith and has an important presence in the assembly. Icons, paintings, and sculpture have a place in the assembly space when they enhance corporate worship and individual devotion.

Background S-16G

The use of flags in our churches received impetus in the early twentieth century when Christians in America wanted to stress their loyalty to this country. A sense of patriotism sometimes leads to the desire to display and honor flags in public places.

Application S-16H

Flags signal national loyalties and may become divisive, implying that a particular national identity is synonymous with the Christian way. Flags, while appropriate in other parts of the church complex and as part of certain national occasions, have no permanent place in the primary Christian worship center.

Part III: Marks of the Worship Environment

Worship space is hospitable

Principle S-17

A hospitable worship space generously accommodates the assembly, its liturgy, and a broad range of activities appropriate to the life of the congregation and its surrounding community.

Application S-17A
Beyond its functional nature, a hospitable space is inviting because of the harmony of its materials, the scale of its proportions, and the integral nature of its parts. Excellent lighting and acoustics, space for liturgical interaction, absence of barriers, and well-crafted furnishings all contribute to hospitality. A hospitable room is not only a good place to worship, it is a good place to be.

Application S-17B
Christian hospitality is reflected in the attention a community gives to making its space physically accessible and welcoming to persons of all ages and abilities. The worship space is life-affirming and promotes physical health and safety as well as mental and spiritual wholeness, honoring the human need for sustenance.

Application S-17C
An understanding of the physical and experiential needs of children contributes to the design of liturgy and liturgical spaces that are inviting to all.

Application S-17D
Christian hospitality is culturally inclusive and recognizes the rich diversity of God's people in dimensions such as gender, race, age, class, ethnic background, and ability. Giving attention to this diversity within the worship space invites the participation of all within the community and speaks to the unity of the body of Christ.

Background S-17E

The synagogue was not only a place for worship but also a place for study and community activity. The first house churches also served many functions for the community. Gradually, the perception developed of church as a holy place reserved for the presence of God. Church structures were built as houses for God instead of houses for the people of God. Even then these buildings continued to be used for a variety of ecclesiastical, personal, and civic functions.

Application S-17F

The multiple use of a worship space serves as a sign of stewardship, ministry, and outreach for a congregation and its surrounding community. Such use need not contradict the primary purpose of the space.

Clarity reveals what is central

Principle S-18

An environment free of nonessentials or the duplication of symbols brings clarity to what is central in worship.

Application S-18A

The presence of God is celebrated in well-defined spaces for baptism, eucharist, and proclamation. The assembly's focus is supported when all elements of the arts and architecture work as a whole to draw attention to the central signs of word and sacrament.

Application S-18B

The essential elements of the liturgical spaces—flowing water, bread, wine, and proclaimed word—become easier for the assembly to experience when care and restraint are exercised in the furnishing and decorating of the liturgical centers, so that the nonessentials do not overshadow the essential elements. The duplication of symbols often leads to their diminution.

Flexibility provides for variety

Principle S-19

Flexibility of space and portability of furniture facilitate the variations of worship as well as related activities of congregation and community.

Background S-19A

Christian liturgy is a dynamic experience. The Sunday eucharist is characterized by movements of ministers and people in processions, the greeting of peace, and gathering around the holy table or other centers of liturgical action. The variations of the liturgical year invite variations in the spatial setting to best express such actions as the lighting of an Advent wreath, Maundy Thursday foot washing, and the movements of the Easter Vigil. Christian burial, marriage, and many other special services require a space that accommodates a variety of needs.

Application S-19B

Flexibility and permanency are held in balance. A foundational component in the room is the baptismal font, acting like an anchor in the space. The altar table can be strong and handsome, like a fine dining table, yet portable. Chairs can be sturdy and beautiful yet moveable, whereas fixed pews often limit the possibilities for physical arrangement of the assembly. A space for musicians can be arranged and rearranged to meet instrumental and choral needs for a given liturgy. Cross, torches, and other furnishings are best designed to be carried, positioned, and repositioned.

Application S-19C

The ability to arrange the furnishings within the worship space in various ways gives a congregation the freedom to adapt as changes and new ideas are introduced.

Beauty opens the assembly to God

Principle S-20

In the worship space, beauty is a portal to the mystery of God and a witness to Christian faith and truth. Beauty is revealed through the honest use of the materials of God's creation.

Background S-20A

Studies in anthropology and comparative religion indicate that people find beauty and mystery in archetypes such as stones, mountains, trees, sky, water, and earth. These elements signal for many people the presence of a creator God and provide an oasis where people can measure their lives against profound patterns of creation. "From the greatness and beauty of created things comes a corresponding perception of their Creator."[110]

Application S-20B

Furniture made of sturdy and beautiful wood, stone or wood sculptures, fabric hangings made of natural fibers, living water and plants, natural light, a loaf of bread, wine, fragrant oil, candles of wax, and the beauty of human forms lead people to an experience of wonder and inspiration that in turn opens them to the mystery of God.

Background S-20C

"Art chosen for the place of worship is not simply something pretty or well made, an addition to make the ordinary more pleasant. . . . Rather, artworks truly belong in the church when they are worthy of the place of worship and when they enhance the liturgical, devotional, and contemplative prayer they are inspired to serve."[111]

Application S-20D

While definitions of beauty vary according to personal or cultural tastes, it is possible to identify some helpful criteria, such as balance and scale, color scheme, and quality materials honestly crafted.

Application S-20E

Original, commissioned artwork can reflect the worship life of a particular congregation. Artists can be nurtured and encouraged in their communities by the incorporation of their art in the worship life of the church.

---

[110] Wisdom of Solomon 13:5.
[111] *Built of Living Stones: Art, Architecture, and Worship* (Washington: United States Catholic Conference, 2000), 29.

Part IV: Renewal of Worship Space and the Community

Liturgical design is an act of prayer

Principle S-21

The process of building a worship space or reordering existing space is itself an act of faith and worship.

Application S-21A

A community of faith is strengthened when planning for the renewal or creation of worship space is intentional and deliberate. Planning includes ample time for education, reflection, experimentation, and research. Congregations benefit from periods of reflection and prayer in what is commonly seen as an educational and administrative enterprise. In prayer they seek the direction and revelation of God in order to shape a vision for the future.

Application S-21B

Preparation to build or renew worship space is strengthened when the community of faith wrestles with the basic theological concepts that have shaped its history and form its current mission and ministry. It is theological conviction, rather than architectural theory, that is the driving force in shaping a house for the church. As part of any building process, a program of congregational education may well explore the meaning and practices of worship, the theological premise behind those practices, and the elements of spatial expression.

The design process involves the whole community

Principle S-22

The whole community of faith is involved in the process of designing and creating a new or renewed worship space.

Application S-22A
Effective planning decisions are made by those who possess the trust and support of the community. Those entrusted with this leadership role reflect the diversity of the congregation and are sufficient in number to establish a common vision. To mark that trust and support the congregation may commission these leaders.

Application S-22B
Visiting and experiencing the liturgy in other places of worship is valuable for all who are engaged in the process of designing liturgical spaces.

Application S-22C
Active dialogue within the congregation enriches the design process and helps to ensure its success. Such conversation leads the community to understand and appreciate the design directions that are undertaken.

Specialists are partners in renewal

Principle S-23

People with training and experience in creating liturgical space are essential partners in renewed use of existing spaces and in new construction projects.

Background S-23A
Liturgical consultants, liturgical designers, architects, engineers, artists, and craftspeople are resource people who can facilitate the work of a congregation. Each has special expertise and a role to play in the process of creating and renewing worship spaces.

Background S-23B
A liturgical consultant enables the community of faith to articulate its theological and liturgical vision and to realize the impact on the environment of worship. The consultant is a teacher of the congregation and those involved in the planning process. The consultant's role enables the architect to set the design process in a solid theological framework. The liturgical consultant has a vital role to play in ensuring that the many voices within the community are heard, and at the same time helping those in the process maintain clear theological vision.

Application S-23C
The work of designers and artisans begins with the worshiping community and is informed in dialogue with the worshiping community.

Application S-23D
The employment of skilled and inspired professionals safeguards not only the material value of design and form, but also the emotional and spiritual resources of the community.

Building is a matter of stewardship

Principle S-24

Choices in its use of money, property, and other resources reflect a community's commitment to service and ministry.

Application S-24A
In selecting building materials, engineering systems, and liturgical appointments, careful consideration for the impact on the environment, the depletion of limited resources, the safety of manufacturing, and the health effects on the building inhabitants will help ensure a place for worship that is life-affirming.

Application S-24B
An understanding of value will ensure the appropriate use of resources and talents in the creation of worship spaces. Value is the appropriate investment of resources into the architecture, furnishings, technology, and liturgical artwork to insure durability, longevity, quality, and significance.

Application S-24C
The responsible creation of a worship space may involve the creative reuse or reconfiguration of building space or furnishings to conserve the treasures of that congregation. Identifying what is worthy of preservation and how to carry out such adaptation is best addressed early in the planning process.

Renewal of spaces encourages renewal of people

Principle S-25

The renewal of a space for worship is an opportunity for the renewal of a worshiping community.

Application S-25A
Building, renovation, and even limited but imaginative renewal projects represent significant experiences in the life of a congregation. From vision to blueprint to implementation, the process is an opportunity for congregational growth in faith and life.

Application S-25B
The journey to understand liturgy, ritual, and liturgical art enriches a community's faith and worship. Even congregations of limited means can undertake modest reordering of their worship space, especially with the assistance of skilled volunteers.

Appendix

The Use of the Means of Grace

A Statement on the Practice of Word and Sacrament

Adopted for guidance and practice by the Fifth Biennial Churchwide Assembly of the Evangelical Lutheran Church in America, August 19, 1997.

Preface: The Triune God and the Means of Grace

The Triune God acts in the means of grace

Principle 1

Jesus Christ is the living and abiding Word of God. By the power of the Spirit, this very Word of God, which is Jesus Christ, is read in the Scriptures, proclaimed in preaching, announced in the forgiveness of sins, eaten and drunk in the Holy Communion, and encountered in the bodily presence of the Christian community. By the power of the Spirit active in Holy Baptism, this Word washes a people to be Christ's own Body in the world. We have called this gift of Word and Sacrament by the name "the means of grace." The living heart of all these means is the presence of Jesus Christ through the power of the Spirit as the gift of the Father.

Background 1A
"We believe we have the duty not to neglect any of the rites and ceremonies instituted in Scripture, whatever their number. We do not think it makes much difference if, for purposes of teaching, the enumeration varies, provided what is handed down in Scripture is preserved. For that matter, the Fathers did not always use the same enumeration."[1]

Background 1B
In Christ's flesh, in his death and resurrection, all people are invited to behold and to receive the fullness of God's grace and truth.[2]

---

[1] Apology of the Augsburg Confession, Article XIII. Note: All citations of confessional material in *The Use of the Means of Grace* are from the *Book of Concord*, translated and edited by Theodore G. Tappert (Philadelphia: Fortress Press, 1959).
[2] John 1:14–16.

The Triune God creates the Church

Principle 2

God gives the Word and the sacraments to the Church and by the power of the Spirit thereby creates and sustains the Church among us.[3] God establishes the sacraments "to awaken and confirm faith."[4] God calls the Church to exercise care and fidelity in its use of the means of grace, so that all people may hear and believe the Gospel of Jesus Christ and be gathered into God's own mission for the life of the world.

Background 2A

In a world of yearning, brokenness, and sin, the Church's clarity about the Gospel of Jesus Christ is vital. God has promised to come to all through the means of grace: the Word and the sacraments of Christ's institution. While the Church defines for itself customary practices that reflect care and fidelity, it is these means of grace that define the Church.

Background 2B

Yet even the Church itself is threatened should it fail to claim the great treasures of the Gospel. Either careless practice or rigid uniformity may distort the power of the gift. This statement is one way in which we, in the Church, can give counsel to one another, supporting and sustaining one another in our common mission.

Background 2C

We are people whose lives are degraded by sin. This estrangement from God manifests itself in many ways, including false values and a sense of emptiness. Many in our time are deprived or depriving, abusing or abused. All humanity, indeed all creation, is threatened by sin that erupts in greed, violence, and war. In the midst of isolation, lovelessness, and self-absorption, the Church is tempted to turn in on itself, its own needs, and preferences. As a church in this time, we seek to give and receive God's Word and sacraments as full and reliable signs of Christ.

---

[3] The Small Catechism, The Creed, The Third Article.
[4] Augsburg Confession, Article XIII.

What is the Church?

Principle 3

"It is also taught among us that one holy Christian church will be and remain forever. This is the assembly of all believers among whom the Gospel is preached in its purity and the holy sacraments are administered according to the Gospel."[5]

Background 3A

The Evangelical Lutheran Church in America is committed by its statement of purpose to "worship God in proclamation of the Word and administration of the sacraments and through lives of prayer, praise, thanksgiving, witness, and service."[6] The Scriptures and our Confessions establish this purpose. We believe that "through the Word and the sacraments, as through means, the Holy Spirit is given, and the Holy Spirit produces faith, where and when it pleases God, in those who hear the Gospel."[7]

This statement encourages unity amid diversity

Principle 4

The gift of Word and Sacrament is from God. This statement on sacramental practices seeks to encourage unity among us in the administration of the means of grace and to foster common understanding and practice. It does not seek to impose uniformity among us.

Background 4A

This statement grows out of this church's concern for healthy pastoral action and strong congregational mission. It does not address our practice of Word and Sacrament out of antiquarian or legalistic interests but rather to ground the practice of our church in the Gospel and to encourage good order within our church.

Application 4B

Our congregations receive and administer the means of grace in richly diverse ways. This diversity in practice is well grounded in the Confessions. "It is not necessary for the true unity of the Christian church that ceremonies of human institution should be observed uniformly in all places."[8] We are united in one common center: Jesus Christ proclaimed in Word and sacraments amidst participating assemblies of singing, serving, and praying people.

---

[5] Augsburg Confession, Article VII.
[6] *Constitution, Bylaws, and Continuing Resolutions of the Evangelical Lutheran Church in America*, 1995, 4.02.
[7] Augsburg Confession, Article V.
[8] Augsburg Confession, Article VII.

Part I: Proclamation of the Word and the Christian Assembly

What is the Word of God?

Principle 5

Jesus Christ is the Word of God incarnate. The proclamation of God's message to us is both Law and Gospel. The canonical Scriptures of the Old and New Testaments are the written Word of God.[9] Through this Word in these forms, as through the sacraments, God gives faith, forgiveness of sins, and new life.

Application 5A
Proclamation of the Word includes the public reading of Scripture, preaching, teaching, the celebration of the sacraments, confession and absolution, music, arts, prayers, Christian witness, and service. The congregation's entire educational ministry participates in the proclamation of the Word.

---

[9] *Constitution, Bylaws, and Continuing Resolutions of the Evangelical Lutheran Church in America*, 2.02.

Sunday provides a day for assembly around Word and Sacrament

Principle 6

Sunday, the day of Christ's resurrection and of the appearances to the disciples by the crucified and risen Christ, is the primary day on which Christians gather to worship. Within this assembly, the Word is read and preached and the sacraments are celebrated.

Application 6A
Sunday is the principal festival day of Christians. The Holy Communion is one name for the Sunday service of Word and Sacrament in which the congregation assembles in God's presence, hears the word of life, baptizes and remembers Baptism, and celebrates the Holy Supper. The service of Word and Sacrament is also celebrated on other great festivals of the year, according to the common Christian calendar received in our churches. The Christian community may gather for proclamation and the Lord's Supper at other times as well, as, for example, on other days of the week, and when the services of marriage or of the burial of the dead are placed within the context of the Holy Communion.[10]

The Scriptures are read aloud

Principle 7

The public reading of the Holy Scriptures is an indispensable part of worship, constituting the basis for the public proclamation of the Gospel.

Application 7A
The use of ELCA–approved lectionaries serves the unity of the Church, the hearing of the breadth of the Scriptures, and the evangelical meaning of the church year. The Revised Common Lectionary and the lectionaries in *Lutheran Book of Worship* make three readings and a psalm available for every Sunday and festival.

Application 7B
The use of a Bible or lectionary of appropriate size and dignity by those who read the Scriptures aloud, the use of this book in liturgical processions, and its placement on the reading desk or pulpit may bring the centrality of the Word to visible expression.

---

[10] *LBW* Ministers Edition (Minneapolis: Augsburg Publishing House, and Philadelphia: Board of Publication, Lutheran Church in America, 1978), 36–37.

The baptized people proclaim God's Word

Principle 8

All the baptized share responsibility for the proclamation of the Word and the formation of the Christian assembly.

Application 8A

One of the ways lay people exercise the public proclamation of the Word is as assisting ministers. Among these assisting ministers will be readers of Scripture and also cantors and leaders of prayer.[11]

Application 8B

Musicians serve the assembly by illuminating the readings and the sacraments, by the congregation's participation in song.

Application 8C

There are varieties of ways beyond the assembly in which the public ministry of the Word is exercised. Some of these include the work of catechists, evangelists, and teachers.

---

[11] *LBW* Ministers Edition, 25. See also principle 41.

God's Word is preached

Principle 9

The preaching of the Gospel of the crucified and risen Christ is rooted in the readings of the Scriptures in the assemblies for worship. Called and ordained ministers bear responsibility for the preached Word in the Church gathered for public worship.[12]

Application 9A
Preaching is the living and contemporary voice of one who interprets in all the Scriptures the things concerning Jesus Christ.[13] In fidelity to the readings appointed for the day, the preacher proclaims our need of God's grace and freely offers that grace, equipping the community for mission and service in daily life. "Only under extraordinary circumstances would the sermon be omitted" from the Sunday and festival service of Holy Communion.[14]

Application 9B
While other persons may sometimes preach, the called pastor of a congregation has responsibility for this preaching, ordinarily preparing and delivering the sermon and overseeing all public ministry of the Word in the congregation. In congregations without a called pastor, the synodical bishop assumes this responsibility, often by providing an interim pastor. All Christians, however, bear responsibility to speak and teach the Gospel in daily life.

[12] See *Baptism, Eucharist and Ministry. Faith and Order Paper No. 111*, (Geneva: World Council of Churches, 1982), Ministry, 8; Augsburg Confession, Article XIV; also *The Study of Ministry Report to the 1991 Assembly: Study Edition* (Chicago: Evangelical Lutheran Church in America, Division for Ministry, 1991).
[13] Luke 24:27.
[14] *LBW* Ministers Edition, 27.

The common voice of the assembly speaks the Word

Principle 10

The assembled congregation participates in proclaiming the Word of God with a common voice. It sings hymns and the texts of the liturgy. It confesses the Nicene or Apostles' Creed.[15]

Application 10A

Hymns, the liturgy, and the creeds are means for the community itself to proclaim and respond to the Word of God.[16] This witness should be valued, taught, and taken to heart. The treasury of music is ever expanding with new compositions and with songs from the churches of the world.

---

[15] The Athanasian Creed is also a confession of the Church, but is rarely used in public worship.
[16] Colossians 3:16.

The arts serve the Word

Principle 11

Music, the visual arts, and the environment of our worship spaces embody the proclamation of the Word in Lutheran churches.

Application 11A

Music is a servant of the Gospel and a principal means of worshiping God in Lutheran churches. Congregational song gathers the whole people to proclaim God's mercy, to worship God, and to pray, in response to the readings of the day and in preparation for the Lord's Supper.

Application 11B

In similar ways the other arts also are called to serve the purposes of the Christian assembly. The visual arts and the spaces for worship assist the congregation to participate in worship, to focus on the essentials, and to embody the Gospel.

Application 11C

In these times of deeper contact among cultures, our congregations do well to make respectful and hospitable use of the music, arts, and furnishings of many peoples. The Spirit of God calls people from every nation, all tribes, peoples, and languages to gather around the Gospel of Jesus Christ.[17]

---

[17] Revelation 7:9.

Confession and Absolution proclaim the Word

Principle 12

The Gospel also is proclaimed in Confession and Absolution (the Office of the Keys) and in the mutual conversation and consolation of the brothers and sisters.[18] Our congregations are called to make faithful use of corporate and individual confession of sins and holy absolution.

Application 12A

Absolution is a speaking and hearing of the Word of God and a return to Baptism. The most important part of confession and forgiveness is the "work which God does, when he absolves me of my sins through a word placed in the mouth" of a human being.[19] Liturgical patterns for corporate and individual confession and forgiveness are given in Lutheran worship books.

On other occasions Christians assemble around the Word

Principle 13

Assemblies for worship are not limited to Sunday or to celebrations of Word and Sacrament. Christians gather for worship on other days of the week, for morning or evening prayer, for services of the Word or devotions, to mark local and national festivals, and for important life occasions such as weddings and funerals. Christians also gather in their own homes for prayer, Bible reading, and devotions.

Application 13A

Every opportunity for worship is valued and encouraged. The communal observance of morning and evening prayer and the celebration of weddings and funerals within services of Word and Sacrament in the congregation are appropriate traditions. Morning and evening prayers and mealtime blessings in the household are also an extension of corporate worship.

---

[18] Smalcald Articles, III., 4.
[19] The Large Catechism, A Brief Exhortation to Confession, 15.

Part II: Holy Baptism and the Christian Assembly

What is Baptism?

Principle 14

In Holy Baptism the Triune God delivers us from the forces of evil, puts our sinful self to death, gives us new birth, adopts us as children, and makes us members of the body of Christ, the Church. Holy Baptism is received by faith alone.

Background 14A

By water and the Word in Baptism, we are liberated from sin and death by being joined to the death and resurrection of Jesus. In Baptism God seals us by the Holy Spirit and marks us with the cross of Christ forever.[20] Baptism inaugurates a life of discipleship in the death and resurrection of Christ. Baptism conforms us to the death and resurrection of Christ precisely so that we repent and receive forgiveness, love our neighbors, suffer for the sake of the Gospel, and witness to Christ.

Application 14B

Baptism is for the sake of life in Christ and in the body of Christ, the Church. It also may be given to those who are close to death, and is a strong word of promise in spite of death. Individuals are baptized, yet this Baptism forms a community. It is for children. It is for adults. It is done once, yet it is for all of our life.

---

[20] See *LBW*, 121, 124.

Jesus Christ has given Holy Baptism

Principle 15

Baptism was given to the Church by Jesus Christ in the Great Commission, but also in his own baptism by John and in the baptism of the cross.

Background 15A

One great source of the teaching and practice of the Church regarding Baptism is the Great Commission: "Go therefore and make disciples of all nations, baptizing them in the name of the Father and of the Son and of the Holy Spirit, and teaching them to obey everything that I have commanded you. And remember, I am with you always, to the end of the age."[21]

Background 15B

Other passages are also part of the biblical tradition of the origin and meaning of Baptism. Another source is the account of Jesus' own baptism at the River Jordan. While Jesus is the eternal Son of God, all who are baptized into him are adopted as beloved children of God. With Jesus all the baptized are anointed by the outpoured Spirit. Because of Jesus we are, through Baptism, gathered and included in the life of the Triune God.

Background 15C

In two places in the New Testament where Jesus speaks of his own baptism,[22] he refers not to his being washed in the Jordan River, but to his impending death.[23] It is that death to which we are joined in Baptism, according to the witness of Paul.[24]

---

[21] Matthew 28:19–20.
[22] Luke 12:50; Mark 10:38.
[23] *The Confirmation Ministry Task Force Report*, Evangelical Lutheran Church in America, 1993, 4.
[24] Romans 6:3.

Baptism is once for all

Principle 16

A person is baptized once. Because of the unfailing nature of God's promise, and because of God's once-for-all action in Christ, Baptism is not repeated.

Background 16A
Baptism is a sign and testimony of God's grace, awakening and creating faith. The faith of the one being baptized "does not constitute Baptism but receives it. . . ." "Everything depends upon the Word and commandment of God. . . ."[25]

Application 16B
Rebaptism is to be avoided[26] since it causes doubt, focusing attention on the always-failing adequacy of our action or our faith. Baptized persons who come to new depth of conviction in faith are invited to an Affirmation of Baptism in the life of the congregation.[27]

Application 16C
There may be occasions when people are uncertain about whether or not they have been baptized. Pastors, after supportive conversation and pastoral discernment, may choose to proceed with the baptism. The practice of this church and its congregations needs to incorporate the person into the community and its ongoing catechesis and to proclaim the sure grace of God in Christ, avoiding any sense of Baptism being repeated.

---

[25] The Large Catechism, Baptism, 53.
[26] *Baptism, Eucharist and Ministry*, Baptism, 13.
[27] The Large Catechism, Baptism, 47–63.

Baptism involves daily dying and rising

Principle 17

By God's gift and call, all of us who have been baptized into Christ Jesus are daily put to death so that we might be raised daily to newness of life.[28]

Background 17A
Believers are at the same time sinners and justified. We experience bondage to sin from which we cannot free ourselves and, at the same time, "rebirth and renewal by the Holy Spirit."[29] The baptismal life is expressed each time the baptized confess their sins and receive forgiveness. "Repentance, therefore, is nothing else than a return and approach to Baptism. . . ."[30]

Application 17B
There are many ways to encourage this daily dying to sin and being raised to live before God. They include confession and absolution, the reading of the Scriptures, preaching, the mutual comfort and consolation of the sisters and brothers,[31] daily prayer and the sign of the cross, the remembrance of the catechism, and the profession of the creed.

Application 17C
Christians continue in the covenant God made with them in Baptism by participation in the community of faith, by hearing the Word and receiving Christ's Supper, by proclaiming the good news in word and deed, and by striving for justice and peace in all the world.[32]

---

[28] The Small Catechism, The Sacrament of Holy Baptism, part four, 12. See also Romans 6.
[29] Titus 3:5.
[30] The Large Catechism, Baptism, 75–90.
[31] Smalcald Articles, III., 4.
[32] *LBW*, 201.

Baptism is for all ages

Principle 18

God, whose grace is for all, is the one who acts in Baptism. Therefore candidates for Baptism are of all ages. Some are adults and older children who have heard the Gospel of Jesus Christ, declare their faith, and desire Holy Baptism. Others are the young or infant children of active members of the congregation or those children for whom members of the congregation assume sponsorship.

Application 18A

Since ancient times, the Christian Church has baptized both infants and adults.[33] Our times require great seriousness about evangelization and readiness to welcome unbaptized adults to the reception of the faith and to Baptism into Christ. Our children also need this sign and means of grace and its continued power in their lives. In either case, Baptism is God's gift of overwhelming grace. We baptize infants as if they were adults, addressing them with questions, words, and promises that their parents, sponsors, and congregation are to help them know and believe as they grow in years. We baptize adults as if they were infants, washing them and clothing them with God's love in Christ.

---

[33] *Baptism, Eucharist and Ministry*, Baptism, 11–12.

Baptism includes catechesis

Principle 19

Baptism includes instruction and nurture in the faith for a life of discipleship.

Application 19A
When infants and young children are baptized, the parents and sponsors receive instruction and the children are taught throughout their development. With adults and older children, the baptismal candidates themselves are given instruction and formation for faith and ministry in the world both prior to and following their baptism. The instruction and formation of sponsors, parents, and candidates prior to Baptism deals especially with faith in the triune God and with prayer. In the case of adults and older children this period of instruction and formation is called the catechumenate. *Occasional Services* includes an order for the enrollment of candidates for Baptism.[34]

Application 19B
The parish education of the congregation is part of its baptismal ministry. Indeed, all of the baptized require lifelong learning, the daily reappropriation of the wonderful gifts given in Baptism.

---

[34] *Occasional Services: A Companion to Lutheran Book of Worship* (Minneapolis: Augsburg Publishing House and Philadelphia: Board of Publication, Lutheran Church in America, 1982), 13–15.

Sponsors assist those being baptized

Principle 20

Both adults and infants benefit from having baptismal sponsors. The primary role of the sponsors is to guide and accompany the candidates and, so far as possible, their families in the process of instruction and Baptism. They help the baptized join in the life and work of the community of believers for the sake of the world.

Application 20A

Congregations are encouraged to select at least one sponsor from among the congregational members for each candidate for Baptism.[35] Additional sponsors who are involved in the faith and life of a Christian community may also be selected by parents of the candidate or by the candidate. Choosing and preparing sponsors requires thoughtful consideration and includes participation by pastors or other congregational leaders.

Background 20B

The sponsors of children are often called godparents. They may fulfill a variety of social roles in certain cultures. The roles may be regarded as an elaboration of the central baptismal role they have undertaken. Such sponsors take on a lifelong task to recall the gifts of Baptism in the life of their godchild.

Background 20C

The sponsor provided by the congregation is, in the case of the baptism of an infant, especially concerned to accompany the family as it prepares for Baptism and, as a mentor, to assist the integration of the child into the community of faith as it grows in years. In the case of the baptism of an adult, this sponsor accompanies the candidate throughout the catechumenate, in prayer and in mutual learning, assisting the newly baptized adult to join in the ministry and mission of this community.

Application 20D

The entire congregation prays for those preparing for Baptism, welcomes the newly baptized, and provides assistance to sponsors.

---

[35] *Statement on Sacramental Practices*, Evangelical Lutheran Church in Canada, 1991.

Baptism takes place in the assembly

Principle 21

Candidates for Holy Baptism, sponsors, and an ordained minister called by the Church gather together with the congregation for the celebration of Baptism within the corporate worship of the Church.

Application 21A
When pastoral considerations require Baptism to take place outside of corporate worship, if at all possible representatives of the congregation gather for Baptism. In such a case a public announcement of the baptism is made at the service the following Sunday.

Application 21B
Baptism may take place at varying points in the worship service. When the Baptism follows the Liturgy of the Word, it helps to emphasize Baptism's connection to the promise of the Gospel and faith in that promise and leads the baptized to the altar. When infants are baptized in a service where adults are not, the Baptism may be part of the entrance rite. This emphasizes that their instruction is to follow and reminds the whole congregation of the baptismal nature of the order for Confession and Forgiveness. At the Vigil of Easter, baptisms are placed between the Service of Readings and the proclamation of the Easter texts. This helps Christians to remember their burial with Christ into death, and rising with him to new life.

A pastor presides at Baptism

Principle 22

An ordained minister presides at Holy Baptism.[36]

Application 22A
God is the one who acts in Baptism. The pastor, congregation, candidates, and sponsors gather around the font to administer the sacrament. The pastor presides in the midst of a participating community. Ordinarily this presider is the pastor of the congregation where the Baptism is being celebrated. The pastor acts as baptizer, but does so within a congregation of the Church which actively assents and responds.

---

[36] *Baptism, Eucharist and Ministry*, Baptism, 22.

Baptism may occur before an imminent death

Principle 23

In cases of imminent death, a person may be baptized by any Christian. Should sudden death prevent Baptism, we commend the person to God with prayer, trusting in God's grace.

Application 23A

Counsel for such a baptism at the time of imminent death may be found in *Occasional Services* and should be widely known in the Christian community.[37] A dead person, child or adult, is not baptized. Prayers at such a death may include naming, signing with the cross, anointing for burial, and commendation to God. Prayers and commendations may be offered in the event of a stillbirth or of the early loss of a pregnancy.

Application 23B

When a person who was baptized in imminent danger of death survives, *Occasional Services* provides for a Public Recognition of the Baptism at corporate worship.[38]

We baptize in the name of the Triune God

Principle 24

Holy Baptism is administered with water in the name of the triune God, Father, Son, and Holy Spirit. Baptism into the name of the triune God involves confessing and teaching the doctrine and meaning of the Trinity. The baptized are welcomed into the body of Christ. This is the community which lives from "the grace of the Lord Jesus Christ, the love of God, and the communion of the Holy Spirit . . . ."[39]

Background 24A

The Church seeks to maintain trinitarian orthodoxy while speaking in appropriate modern language and contexts. While a worldwide ecumenical discussion is now underway about such language, we have no other name in which to baptize than the historic and ecumenically received name.[40]

---

[37] *Occasional Services*, 16–22.
[38] *Occasional Services*, 17–22.
[39] 2 Corinthians 13:13.
[40] *Baptism, Eucharist and Ministry*, Baptism, 17.

Background 24B

It is in the crucified Jesus that we meet the God to whom he entrusted all, who raised him from the dead for us, and who poured out the Spirit from his death and resurrection. Washing with water in this name is much more than the use of a formula. The name is a summary of the power and presence of the triune God and of that teaching which must accompany every Baptism. Without this teaching and without the encounter with the grace, love, and communion of the triune God, the words may be misunderstood as a magic formula or as a misrepresentation of the one God in three persons, "equal in glory, coeternal in majesty."[41] What *Father* and *Son* mean, in biblical and creedal perspective, must also be continually reexamined. The doctrine of God teaches us the surprising theology of the cross and counters "any alleged Trinitarian sanction for sinful inequality or oppression of women in church and society."[42]

Application 24C

Some Christians, however, are received into our congregations from other churches in which they were baptized "in the name of Jesus Christ."[43] There are some whose Baptisms were accompanied by trinitarian examination and confession of faith,[44] and whose Baptisms have occurred within the context of trinitarian life and teaching. We will do well to avoid quarrels over the validity of these Baptisms.

Application 24D

Outside the context of trinitarian life and teaching no Christian Baptism takes place, whatever liturgical formula may be used.

---

[41] Athanasian Creed.
[42] Action of the Conference of Bishops, March 8–11, 1991, Evangelical Lutheran Church in America.
[43] Acts 2:38.
[44] Apostolic Tradition of Hippolytus, 21.

Baptism is a public sign

Principle 25

We seek to celebrate Baptism in such a way that the celebration is a true and complete sign of the things which Baptism signifies.[45]

Background 25A

"The pedagogical force of practice is considerable."[46] A strong baptismal theology calls for a strong baptismal practice, teaching and showing forth the meaning of Baptism and inviting Christians to discover continually its importance for their daily lives. Those who plan baptisms attend to the use of faithful words and gracious actions, to including the event within the Sunday service, to the architectural or natural setting, to the regular preparation of candidates, sponsors, parents, and congregation for Baptism, to post-baptismal teaching that strengthens us for mission, and to the possibility of great festivals as times for Baptism.

Application 25B

"It is appropriate to designate such occasions as the Vigil of Easter, the Day of Pentecost, All Saints' Day, and the Baptism of Our Lord for the celebration of Holy Baptism. Baptismal celebrations on these occasions keep Baptism integrated into the unfolding of the story of salvation provided by the church year."[47] The Vigil of Easter is an especially ancient and appropriate time for Baptism, emphasizing the origin of all baptism in Christ's death and resurrection.

---

[45] Martin Luther, "The Holy and Blessed Sacrament of Baptism," 1, in *Luther's Works,* 35:29.
[46] *The Sacrament of the Altar and Its Implications*, United Lutheran Church in America, 1960, C.5.
[47] *LBW* Ministers Edition, 30; see *Baptism, Eucharist and Ministry*, Baptism, 23.

Water is used generously

Principle 26

Water is a sign of cleansing, dying, and new birth.[48] It is used generously in Holy Baptism to symbolize God's power over sin and death.

Application 26a

A variety of modes may be used; for example, both immersion and pouring show forth God's power in Baptism. Immersion helps to communicate the dying and rising with Christ. Pouring suggests cleansing from sin. We have taught that it is not the water which does such great things, but the Word of God connected with the water.[49] God can use whatever water we have. Yet, with Martin Luther, we wish to make full use of water, when it is possible. "For baptism . . . signifies that the old man [self] and the sinful birth of flesh and blood are to be wholly drowned by the grace of God. We should therefore do justice to its meaning and make baptism a true and complete sign of the thing it signifies."[50]

A font is located in the assembly

Principle 27

A baptismal font filled with water, placed in the assembly's worship space, symbolizes the centrality of this sacrament for faith and life.

Application 27a

As congregations are able, they may consider the creation of fonts of ample proportions filled with flowing water, or baptismal pools which could allow immersion. "The location of the font within the church building should express the idea of entrance into the community of faith, and should allow ample space for people to gather around."[51]

---

[48] *LBW*, 122.
[49] The Small Catechism, part four.
[50] Martin Luther, "The Holy and Blessed Sacrament of Baptism," 1, in *Luther's Works*, 35:29.
[51] *LBW* Ministers Edition, 30.

Other signs proclaim the meanings of Baptism

Principle 28

The laying on of hands and prayer for the Holy Spirit's gifts, the signing with the cross, and the anointing with oil help to appropriate the breadth of meanings in Baptism. Other symbolic acts also are appropriate such as the clothing with a baptismal garment and the giving of a lighted candle.

Background 28A

These interpretive signs proclaim the gifts that are given by the promise of God in Baptism itself. Some keys to their interpretation are given in the Holy Scriptures. The laying on of both hands with the prayer for the gifts of the Holy Spirit is a sign of the pouring out of the Spirit of God to empower the people of God for mission. The sign of the cross marks the Christian as united with the Crucified. The use of oil is a sign of anointing with the Spirit and of union with Jesus Christ, the anointed one of God.

Baptism incorporates into the Church

Principle 29

In Baptism people become members not only of the Church universal but of a particular congregation. Therefore all baptisms are entered into the permanent records of the congregation and certificates are issued at the time of the administration of the sacrament.

Application 29A

The time of the presentation of this certificate may be at the Baptism itself or at a post-baptismal visit or during post-baptismal formation. The Evangelical Lutheran Church in America keeps a roster from the baptismal ministry of its military chaplains.

Baptism is repeatedly affirmed

Principle 30

The public rite for Affirmation of Baptism may be used at many times in the life of a baptized Christian. It is especially appropriate at Confirmation and at times of reception or restoration into membership.

Application 30A
"When there are changes in a Christian's life, rites of affirmation of Baptism and intercessory prayer could mark the passage."[52] "Moving into a nursing home, beginning parenthood or grandparenthood, choosing or changing an occupation, moving out of the parental home, the diagnosis of a chronic illness, the end of one's first year of mourning, the ending of a relationship, and retirement are all examples of life's transitions that could be acknowledged by these rites."[53] Other examples include adoption and the naming of an already baptized child, release from prison, reunion of an immigrant family, and new life after abuse or addiction.

Application 30B
Every Baptism celebrated in the assembly is an occasion for the remembrance and renewal of baptism on the part of all the baptized. The Easter Vigil especially provides for a renewal of baptism.[54]

---

[52] *The Confirmation Ministry Task Force Report*, 9–10.
[53] *The Confirmation Ministry Task Force Report*, 9–10.
[54] *LBW* Ministers Edition, 152.

Part III: Holy Communion and the Christian Assembly

What is Holy Communion?

Principle 31

At the table of our Lord Jesus Christ, God nourishes faith, forgives sin, and calls us to be witnesses to the Gospel.

Background 31A
Here we receive Christ's body and blood and God's gifts of forgiveness of sin, life, and salvation to be received by faith for the strengthening of faith.[55]

Jesus Christ has given the Holy Communion

Principle 32

The Lord's Supper was instituted by Jesus Christ on the night of his betrayal.[56]

Background 32A
In numerous places in the Gospels, the early Church also recognized the eucharistic significance of other meals during Christ's ministry and after his resurrection.[57]

---

[55] The Small Catechism, and Augsburg Confession XIII.2.
[56] Matthew 26:26–29 and parallels; 1 Corinthians 11:23–24.
[57] See, for example, Mark 6:30–52 and parallels, Luke 24:13–35.

Jesus Christ is truly present in this sacrament

Principle 33

In this sacrament the crucified and risen Christ is present, giving his true body and blood as food and drink. This real presence is a mystery.

Background 33A

The Augsburg Confession states: "It is taught among us that the true body and blood of Christ are really present in the Supper of our Lord under the form of bread and wine and are there distributed and received."[58] The Apology of the Augsburg Confession adds: "We are talking about the presence of the living Christ, knowing that 'death no longer has dominion over him.'"[59]

Background 33B

"The 'how' of Christ's presence remains as inexplicable in the sacrament as elsewhere. It is a presence that remains 'hidden' even though visible media are used in the sacrament. The earthly element is . . . a fit vehicle of the divine presence and it, too, the common stuff of our daily life, participates in the new creation which has already begun."[60]

---

[58] Augsburg Confession, Article X.
[59] Apology of the Augsburg Confession, Article XXIV.
[60] *The Sacrament of the Altar and Its Implications*, United Lutheran Church in America, 1960.

The celebration of Holy Communion includes both Word and sacramental meal

Principle 34

The two principal parts of the liturgy of Holy Communion, the proclamation of the Word of God and the celebration of the sacramental meal, are so intimately connected as to form one act of worship.

Application 34A

Our congregations are encouraged to hold these two parts together, avoiding either a celebration of the Supper without the preceding reading of the Scriptures, preaching, and intercessory prayers or a celebration of the Supper for a few people who remain after the dismissal of the congregation from a Service of the Word. The Holy Communion is not simply appended to the offices of Morning or Evening Prayer.

Application 34B

The simple order of our liturgy of Holy Communion, represented in the worship books of our church, is that which has been used by generations of Christians. We gather in song and prayer, confessing our need of God. We read the Scriptures and hear them preached. We profess our faith and pray for the world, sealing our prayers with a sign of peace. We gather an offering for the poor and for the mission of the Church. We set our table with bread and wine, give thanks and praise to God, proclaiming Jesus Christ, and eat and drink. We hear the blessing of God and are sent out in mission to the world.

The Holy Communion is celebrated weekly

Principle 35

According to the Apology of the Augsburg Confession,[61] Lutheran congregations celebrate the Holy Communion every Sunday and festival. This confession remains the norm for our practice.

Background 35A
The Church celebrates the Holy Communion frequently because the Church needs the sacrament, the means by which the Church's fellowship is established and its mission as the baptized people of God is nourished and sustained.[62] This practice was reaffirmed in 1989 by the Evangelical Lutheran Church in America. We continue to need "consistent pastoral encouragement and instruction relating to Holy Communion . . . pointing up Christ's command, his promise, and our deep need."[63] For a variety of historical reasons, Lutherans in various places moved away from the weekly celebration of the sacrament.

Application 35B
All of our congregations are encouraged to celebrate the Lord's Supper weekly, but not every service need be a Eucharist.

Application 35C
Participation in the sacramental meal is by invitation, not demand. The members of this church are encouraged to make the sacrament a frequent rather than an occasional part of their lives.

[61] Apology of the Augsburg Confession, Article XXIV.
[62] "The Grace-full Use of the Means of Grace: Theses on Worship and Worship Practices," Lutheran members of the North American Academy of Liturgy, 1994, 28.
[63] A Statement on Communion Practices, ELCA, 1989, II.B.2. (Identical to 1978 statement of predecessor church bodies.)

The Holy Communion has a variety of names

Principle 36

A variety of names demonstrate the richness of Holy Communion. Those names include the Lord's Supper, Holy Communion, Eucharist, Mass, the Sacrament of the Altar, the Divine Liturgy, and the Divine Service.

Background 36A

Each name has come to emphasize certain aspects of the sacrament. The *Lord's Supper* speaks of the meal which the risen Lord holds with the Church, the meal of the Lord's Day, a foretaste of the heavenly feast to come. *Holy Communion* accentuates the holy *koinonia* (community) established by the Holy Spirit as we encounter Christ and are formed into one body with him and so with each other. *Eucharist* calls us to see that the whole meal is a great thanksgiving for creation and for creation's redemption in Jesus Christ. *Divine Liturgy* says the celebration is a public action, carried out by a community of people. Yet, *Divine Service* helps us to see that the primary action of our gathering is God's astonishing service to us; we are called to respond in praise and in service to our neighbor. The term *Mass* is probably derived from the old dismissal of the participants at the end of the service and the sending away of the bread and the cup to the absent: it invites us into mission. *Sacrament of the Altar* invites each one to eat and drink from the true altar of God, the body and blood of Christ given and shed "for you."[64]

---

[64] "The Grace-full Use of the Means of Grace: Theses on Worship and Worship Practices," 27.

The Holy Communion is given to the baptized

Principle 37

Admission to the Sacrament is by invitation of the Lord, presented through the Church to those who are baptized.[65]

Application 37A

When adults and older children are baptized, they may be communed for the first time in the service in which they are baptized. Baptismal preparation and continuing catechesis include instruction for Holy Communion.

Background 37B

Customs vary on the age and circumstances for admission to the Lord's Supper. The age for communing children continues to be discussed and reviewed in our congregations. When "A Report on the Study of Confirmation and First Communion"[66] was adopted, a majority of congregations now in the Evangelical Lutheran Church in America separated confirmation and reception of Holy Communion and began inviting children to commune in the fifth grade. Since that time a number of congregations have continued to lower the age of communion, especially for school age children. Although *A Statement on Communion Practices*[67] precluded the communion of infants, members and congregations have become aware of this practice in some congregations of this church, in historical studies of the early centuries of the Church, in the Evangelical Lutheran Church in Canada, and in broader ecumenical discussion.

Application 37C

Baptized children begin to commune on a regular basis at a time determined through mutual conversation that includes the pastor, the child, and the parents or sponsors involved, within the accepted practices of the congregation. Ordinarily this beginning will occur only when children can eat and drink, and can start to respond to the gift of Christ in the Supper.

Application 37D

Infants and children may be communed for the first time during the service in which they are baptized or they may be brought to the altar during communion to receive a blessing.

---

[65] *A Statement on Communion Practices*, 1989, II.A.2.
[66] "A Report on the Study of Confirmation and First Communion by Lutheran Congregations," Joint Lutheran Commission on the Theology and Practice of Confirmation. (Philadelphia: Lutheran Church in America, 1969).
[67] *A Statement on Communion Practices*, 1989, II.A.2.

Application 37E

In all cases, participation in Holy Communion is accompanied by catechesis appropriate to the age of the communicant. When infants and young children are communed, the parents and sponsors receive instruction and the children are taught throughout their development.

Background 37F

Catechesis, continuing throughout the life of the believer, emphasizes the sacrament as gift, given to faith by and for participation in the community. Such faith is not simply knowledge or intellectual understanding but trust in God's promises given in the Lord's Supper ("for you" and "for the forgiveness of sin") for the support of the baptized.

Application 37G

When an unbaptized person comes to the table seeking Christ's presence and is inadvertently communed, neither that person nor the ministers of Communion need be ashamed. Rather, Christ's gift of love and mercy to all is praised. That person is invited to learn the faith of the Church, be baptized, and thereafter faithfully receive Holy Communion.

The age of first Communion may vary

Principle 38

Common mission among the congregations of this church depends on mutual respect for varied practice in many areas of church life including the ages of first Communion.

Background 38A

"In faithful participation in the mission of God in and through this church, congregations, synods, and the churchwide organization—as interdependent expressions of this church—shall be guided by the biblical and confessional commitments of this church. Each shall recognize that mission efforts must be shaped by both local needs and global awareness, by both individual witness and corporate endeavor, and by both distinctly Lutheran emphases and growing ecumenical cooperation."[68]

---

[68] *Constitution, Bylaws, and Continuing Resolutions of the Evangelical Lutheran Church in America,* 8.16.

Background 38B

There is no command from our Lord regarding the age at which people should be baptized or first communed. Our practice is defined by Christ's command ("Do this"), Christ's twin promises of his presence for us and for our need, and the importance of good order in the Church. In all communion practices congregations strive to avoid both reducing the Lord's Supper to an act effective by its mere performance without faith and narrowing faith to intellectual understanding of Christ's presence and gifts. Congregations continually check their own practices and statements against these biblical and confessional guides.

Application 38C

Congregations of this church may establish policies regarding the age of admission to Holy Communion. They also may grant pastoral exceptions to those policies in individual cases which honor and serve the interdependence (*koinonia*) of congregations of this church.

Application 38D

Out of mutual respect among congregations, children who are communing members of a congregation of this church who move to a congregation with a different practice should be received as communing members (perhaps as a pastoral exception to the congregation's general policy). They and their parents also should be respectful of the traditions and practices of their new congregation. Even if transferring children have received education appropriate to their age in a former parish, the new congregation's program of instruction is also to be followed.

The Holy Communion takes place in the assembly

Principle 39

The gathered people of God celebrate the sacrament. Holy Communion, usually celebrated within a congregation, also may be celebrated in synodical, churchwide, and other settings where the baptized gather.

Application 39A
Authorization for all celebrations of Communion in a parish setting where there is a called and ordained minister of Word and Sacrament is the responsibility of the pastor in consultation with the Congregation Council.

Application 39B
In established centers of this church—e.g., seminaries, colleges, retreat centers, charitable institutions, and administrative centers— authorization for the celebration of Holy Communion shall be given, either for a limited or unlimited time, by the presiding bishop of this church or, where only one synod is concerned, by the bishop of that synod.

Application 39C
In institutions not formally associated with this church—e.g., hospitals, retirement homes, colleges and universities, or military bases—where there is a called pastor or chaplain, authorization for the celebration of Holy Communion rests with the pastor in consultation with the appropriate calling-sending expression of this church.[69]

Background 39D
The authorizing role of bishops is a sign of our interconnectedness. This church provides for ministry in many settings. Chaplains, for example, bring the means of grace to people in institutions on behalf of the whole Church.

[69] *A Statement on Communion Practices*, 1989, II.A.6. See also churchwide continuing resolution 7.44.A96 on the "Table of Sources of Calls for Ordained Ministers."

A pastor presides at the Holy Communion

Principle 40

In witness that this sacrament is a celebration of the Church, serving its unity, an ordained minister presides in the service of Holy Communion and proclaims the Great Thanksgiving. Where it is not possible for an extended period of time to provide ordained pastoral leadership, a synodical bishop may authorize a properly trained lay person to preside for a specified period of time and in a given location only.[70]

Background 40A

"In the celebration of the eucharist, Christ gathers, teaches and nourishes the church. It is Christ who invites to the meal and who presides at it. He is the shepherd who leads the people of God, the prophet who announces the Word of God, the priest who celebrates the mystery of God. In most churches, this presidency is signified by an ordained minister. The one who presides at the eucharistic celebration in the name of Christ makes clear that the rite is not the assembly's own creation or possession; the eucharist is received as a gift from Christ living in his church. The minister of the eucharist is the ambassador who represents the divine initiative and expresses the connection of the local community with other local communities in the universal Church."[71]

[70] *Constitutions, Bylaws, and Continuing Resolutions of the Evangelical Lutheran Church in America*, 7.61.01.
[71] *Baptism, Eucharist and Ministry*, Eucharist, 29.

Lay assisting ministers serve in many roles

Principle 41

Designated and trained lay persons serve in a variety of leadership roles in the Eucharist. Among these assisting ministers will be readers, interpreters, cantors, musicians and choir members, servers of communion, acolytes, leaders of prayer, those who prepare for the meal, and those who offer hospitality.[72]

Background 41A

"The liturgy is the celebration of all who gather. Together with the pastor who presides, the entire congregation is involved. It is important, therefore, that lay persons fulfill appropriate ministries within the service."[73]

---

[72] See also application 8A.
[73] *LBW* Ministers Edition, 25.

Preparation is recommended

Principle 42

Forms of preparation for Holy Communion focus the community of faith both on the breadth of creation's need for redemption and the depth of God's redemptive actions. Such forms of preparation are recommended, but not required, for that person "is worthy and well prepared who believes these words, 'for you' and 'for the forgiveness of sins.'"[74]

Application 42A

Opportunities for corporate and individual confession and absolution, including the use of the Brief Order for Confession and Forgiveness, are especially appropriate. Helpful forms of personal preparation may include self-examination, prayer, fasting, meditation, and reconciliation with others through the exchange of peace.

Background 42B

In considering preparation for Holy Communion many people in our congregations have turned for counsel to Paul's admonition to the Corinthians: "Examine yourselves, and only then eat of the bread and drink of the cup. For all who eat and drink without discerning the body eat and drink judgment against themselves."[75] Paul's words are addressed to those in the community who are eating and drinking while excluding from the meal others who belong to Christ. "Do you show contempt for the church of God," he says, "and humiliate those who have nothing?"[76] The body that Christians need to discern is the body of Christ which is the Church[77] and that is the body which is being ignored by the exclusions in Corinth.

---

[74] The Small Catechism, Article VI. Formula of Concord, Solid Declaration VII., 68–69.
[75] 1 Corinthians 11:28–29.
[76] 1 Corinthians 11:22.
[77] 1 Corinthians 12.

The Holy Communion is consecrated by the Word of God and prayer

Principle 43

The biblical words of institution declare God's action and invitation. They are set within the context of the Great Thanksgiving. This eucharistic prayer proclaims and celebrates the gracious work of God in creation, redemption, and sanctification.

Application 43A

Our worship books provide several options for giving thanks at the table of the Lord. All of them begin with the dialogue of invitation to thanksgiving and conclude with the Lord's Prayer. Most of them include the preface and the Sanctus after the dialogue. Many continue with an evangelical form of the historic prayer after the Sanctus. The full action, from dialogue through the Lord's Prayer, including the proclamation of the words of institution, is called the Great Thanksgiving. Our congregations, synods, and churchwide organization are encouraged to use these patterns of thanksgiving.[78]

---

[78] Apology of the Augsburg Confession, Article XXIV., 76.

Bread and wine are used

Principle 44

In accordance with the words of institution, this church uses bread and wine in the celebration of the Lord's Supper. Communicants normally receive both elements, bread and wine, in the Holy Communion.

Application 44A

A loaf of bread and a chalice are encouraged since they signify the unity which the sacrament bestows. The bread may be leavened or unleavened. The wine may be white or red.

Background 44B

The use of leavened bread is the most ancient attested practice of the Church and gives witness to the connection between the Eucharist and ordinary life. Unleavened bread underscores the Passover themes which are present in the biblical accounts of the Last Supper.

Application 44C

For pressing reasons of health, individuals may commune under one element. In certain circumstances, congregations might decide to place small amounts of non-wheat bread or nonalcoholic wine or grape juice on the altar. Such pastoral and congregational decisions are delicate, and must honor both the tradition of the Church and the people of each local assembly.

Background 44D

Some communicants suffer from allergic reactions or are recovering from alcoholism. As suggested by the 1989 Evangelical Lutheran Church in America *A Statement on Communion Practices*,[79] it is appropriate for them to receive only one of the elements. Their pastor may assure them that the crucified and risen Christ is fully present for them in, with, and under this one element. While our confessions speak against Communion "in one form,"[80] their intent is to protest the practice of withholding the cup from the whole assembly. The confessional concern is to make both the bread and the wine of the sacrament available to the faithful, and not to inhibit them.

---

[79] *A Statement on Communion Practices*, 1989, II.C.3.
[80] See Smalcald Articles, III., 6.

Communion practices reflect unity and dignity

Principle 45

Practices of distributing and receiving Holy Communion reflect the unity of the Body of Christ and the dignity and new life of the baptized.

Application 45A
The promise of Christ is spoken to each communicant by those distributing the Sacrament: "The Body of Christ given for you;" "The Blood of Christ shed for you." Ordinarily the bread is placed in the communicant's hand and the chalice is guided by the communicant or carefully poured by the minister of communion.

Application 45B
Continuous communion of the whole congregation, with the post-communion blessing given after all have communed, underscores the aspects of fellowship and unity in the sacrament. Either standing or kneeling is appropriate when receiving Communion.[81] Ministers of Communion will need to facilitate the communion of those who have difficulty moving, kneeling, standing, holding the bread, or guiding the chalice.

Application 45C
Common devotion during the distribution of Communion is served both by music and by silence.

---

[81] *A Statement on Communion Practices*, 1989, II.C.3.

Leaders commune at each service

Principle 46

As a sign of unity, and out of their own need for grace, the presiding minister and assisting ministers may commune at each Eucharist.

Application 46A
"It is appropriate within the Lutheran tradition that the presiding minister commune himself/herself or receive the Sacrament from an assistant."[82] This reception may be before or after the congregation communes.

The bread and wine are handled with reverence

Principle 47

The bread and wine of Communion are handled with care and reverence, out of a sense of the value both of what has been set apart by the Word as a bearer of the presence of Christ and of God's good creation.

Application 47A
The food needed for the sacramental meal is placed on the table before the Great Thanksgiving. This is done so that the gathered assembly may see the full sign of the food it is to share, and so that we may give thanks and proclaim God's promise in conjunction with the use of this very bread and wine. Nonetheless, in the rare event that more of either element is needed during distribution, it is not necessary to repeat the words of institution.[83]

Application 47B
Any food that remains is best consumed by the presiding and assisting ministers and by others present following the service.

---

[82] *A Statement on Communion Practices*, 1989, II.C.3.
[83] *A Statement on Communion Practices*, 1989, II.C.2.

Congregations provide Communion for the absent

Principle 48

Congregations provide for communion of the sick, homebound, and imprisoned.

Application 48A
Occasional Services provides an order for the Distribution of Communion to Those in Special Circumstances. As an extension of the Sunday worship, the servers of Communion take the elements to those unable to attend.[84]

Application 48B
When pastors celebrate a service of Word and Sacrament in a home, hospital, or other institution, the corporate nature of the gift is strengthened by including others from the congregation. *Occasional Services* provides an order for the Celebration of Holy Communion with Those in Special Circumstances.[85]

---

[84] *Occasional Services,* 76–82.
[85] *Occasional Services,* 83–88.

We practice eucharistic hospitality

Principle 49

Believing in the real presence of Christ, this church practices eucharistic hospitality. All baptized persons are welcomed to Communion when they are visiting in the congregations of this church.

Application 49A

Admission to the sacrament is by invitation of the Lord, presented through the Church to those who are baptized.[86] It is a sign of hospitality to provide a brief written or oral statement in worship which teaches Christ's presence in the sacrament. This assists guests to decide whether they wish to accept the Lord's invitation. In the exercise of this hospitality, it is wise for our congregations to be sensitive to the eucharistic practices of the churches from which visitors may come.

Application 49B

When a wedding or a funeral occurs during a service of Holy Communion, communion is offered to all baptized persons.

---

[86] *A Statement on Communion Practices*, 1989, II.A.2.

Lutherans long for unity at Christ's table

Principle 50

Because of the universal nature of the Church, Lutherans may participate in the eucharistic services of other Christian churches.

Background 50A
This church's ongoing ecumenical dialogues continue to seek full communion with other Christian churches.

Application 50B
When visiting other churches Lutherans should respect the practices of the host congregation. A conscientious decision whether or not to commune in another church is informed by the Lutheran understanding of the Gospel preached and the sacraments administered as Christ's gift.

Application 50C
For Lutheran clergy to be involved as presiding or assisting ministers in the celebration of Holy Communion in other churches, a reciprocal relationship between the denominations involved should prevail.[87]

---

[87] *A Statement on Communion Practices,* 1989, II.A.7.

Part IV: The Means of Grace and Christian Mission

The means of grace lead the Church to mission

Principle 51

In every celebration of the means of grace, God acts to show forth both the need of the world and the truth of the Gospel. In every gathering of Christians around the proclaimed Word and the holy sacraments, God acts to empower the Church for mission. Jesus Christ, who is God's living bread come down from heaven, has given his flesh to be the life of the world.[88] This very flesh, given for the life of all, is encountered in the Word and sacraments.

Background 51A

Baptism and baptismal catechesis join the baptized to the mission of Christ. Confession and absolution continually reconcile the baptized to the mission of Christ. Assembly itself, when that assembly is an open invitation to all peoples to gather around the truth and presence of Jesus Christ, is a witness in the world. The regular proclamation of both Law and Gospel, in Scripture reading and in preaching, tells the truth about life and death in all the world, calls us to faith in the life-giving God, and equips the believers for witness and service. Intercessory prayer makes mention of the needs of all the world and of all the Church in mission. When a collection is received, it is intended for the support of mission and for the concrete needs of our neighbors who are sick, hurt, and hungry. The holy Supper both feeds us with the body and blood of Christ and awakens our care for the hungry ones of the earth. The dismissal from the service sends us in thanksgiving from what we have seen in God's holy gifts to service in God's beloved world.

Application 51B

In the teaching and practice of congregations, the missional intention for the means of grace needs to be recalled. By God's gift, the Word and the sacraments are set in the midst of the world, for the life of the world.[89]

---

[88] John 6:51.
[89] John 1:14; Matthew 28:19; John 10:10.

Baptism comes to expression in Christian vocation

Principle 52

Christians profess baptismal faith as they engage in discipleship in the world. God calls Christians to use their various vocations and ministries to witness to the Gospel of Christ wherever they serve or work.

Background 52A

"As baptized people, we see our daily life as a place to carry out our vocation, our calling. All aspects of life, home and school, community and nation, daily work and leisure, citizenship and friendship, belong to God. All are places where God calls us to serve. God's Word and the church help us to discover ways to carry out our calling."[90]

Application 52B

Teaching about vocation and opportunities for witness and service play an important role in the preparation of adults for Baptism and in post-baptismal catechesis for both adults and children.

The Word of God leads Christians to lived prayer

Principle 53

Because of the living Word of God, Christian assemblies for worship are occasions for intercessory prayer. On the grounds of the Word and promise of God the Church prays, in the power of the Spirit and in the name of Jesus Christ, for all the great needs of the world.

Application 53A

Intercessory prayer is one of the ways that Christians exercise the priesthood of all the baptized. In the Sunday service, such prayer is appropriately led by a lay assisting minister. This prayer is also lived. Christians are called and empowered by the triune God to be a presence of faith, hope, and love in the midst of the needs of the community and the world.

---

[90] *The Confirmation Ministry Task Force Report*, 5; *Together for Ministry: Final Report and Recommendations of the Task Force on the Study of Ministry*, 1993, 15–16.

The Holy Communion strengthens us to witness and to work for justice

Principle 54

As a means of grace Holy Communion is that messianic banquet at which God bestows mercy and forgiveness, creates and strengthens faith for our daily work and ministry in the world, draws us to long for the day of God's manifest justice in all the world, and provides a sure and certain hope of the coming resurrection to eternal life.

Background 54A

Christian eschatology, the teaching that God has an intention and a goal for all the beloved created universe, belongs to the celebration of Holy Communion and to the catechesis of all communicants. This Supper forms the Church, as a community, to bear witness in the world. Our need to be nourished and sustained in this mission is one principal reason for the frequent celebration of the sacrament.

Application 54B

"When you have partaken of this sacrament, therefore, or desire to partake of it, you must in turn share the misfortunes of the fellowship, . . . Here your heart must go out in love and learn that this is a sacrament of love. As love and support are given to you, you in turn must render love and support to Christ in his needy ones. You must feel with sorrow all the dishonor done to Christ in his holy Word, all the misery of Christendom, all the unjust suffering of the innocent, with which the world is everywhere filled to overflowing. You must fight, work, pray, and—if you cannot do more—have heartfelt sympathy. . . . It is Christ's will, then, that we partake of it frequently, in order that we may remember him and exercise ourselves in this fellowship according to his example."[91]

---

[91] Martin Luther, "The Blessed Sacrament of the Holy and True Body of Christ, and the Brotherhoods," 9,12, in *Luther's Works*, 35:54, 56–57.

Principles
for Worship

Study and Response

Study and Response

The publication of *Principles for Worship* in the Renewing Worship series of provisional resources is intended to encourage study throughout the church about the understandings and practice of Christian worship. The following study guide may be used in conjunction with the principles as a basis for study and conversation within congregations and in other settings. Congregations and individuals may use the form at the end of this section to respond to the principles regarding language, music, preaching, and worship space. All responses are welcomed and will be considered as the church continues to renew and deepen its worship life.

Note to the Study Leader

As leader, you play an important role in this study. A study leader is responsible to plan the sessions, make sure resources are available to participants, guide the discussion in order to cover the material, encourage participation by all, help summarize learning, and help carry through on any possible actions that may arise from your study. You do not need to be a pastor or church professional to lead this study, but some previous study of worship in word and sacrament will be helpful.

Purpose of Your Study

Your study may seek to accomplish one or both of the following goals:

1. That those who study may understand the principles with their background and applications, especially in light of the local congregational setting, and consider how they might inform the renewal of worship in the congregation.

2. That those who study may offer a constructive response to the newly-developed principles so that the wider church's guidance about worship matters may be shaped and enriched.

Note: Any suggestions for change in the worship life of the congregation that result from this study should be forwarded to the congregation's worship committee, if such a committee exists, or to the congregation council for possible action.

Caution: Any suggestions to change the manner in which a congregation worships may be seen as a threat by some. Many people treasure the comfortable repetition that a community's worship often becomes. Careful communication and intentional preparation regarding new or modified worship practices are essential to a congregation's acceptance of change as a meaningful renewal of its worship life. Assure everyone that any suggested changes would be carried out only after thorough study and with the affirmation of the congregation through its processes of decision-making.

Audience

Principles for Worship is meant to enrich the worship life of congregations. An important beginning towards this goal will happen when groups of individuals in congregations come together to study the principles and to think through their implications for the congregation and the church at large. Any group of youth and/or adults in the congregation can benefit from a study of the principles. Those who have responsibility for the worship life of the congregation—such as the worship committee, the congregation council, and the altar guild—will find such a study especially important to their work.

Preparation

Be sure you have a copy of the principles (or the major section that you will be studying) for each participant. Making these available before your first session and encouraging all to read in advance will enrich your discussion.

You might assign one person to lead opening and closing prayers.

You might assign a set or group of principles to individual participants (or participants working in pairs). Encourage participants to become as familiar as possible with the principles they have been assigned. They might do additional research on the principles, write or summarize the principles in their own words, interview people in the congregation about the principles, write discussion questions relating to the principles, or bring someone to your class session who has expertise in the area that the principles cover.

Invite the congregation's pastor, the director of music, or others who could enrich your discussion, especially during specific sessions.

Plan ways of including children and young people in the discussion about worship.

Be sure to include some who have a long history in the Lutheran church or in your congregation. Their memories can enrich your discussion.

Session Plans

Principles for Worship consists of four chapters, each with 15-25 principles and their corresponding background and application statements. First, read over the whole document and mark those principles that seem most relevant to your congregation. Your choices will help you plan how to go about your study.

Decide how many sessions you will be able to dedicate to this study. You might, for example, decide on six one-hour sessions, one each for language, music, preaching, and worship space, in addition to a session on the introduction and a concluding session. In this case, you will probably need to select a smaller number of principles in each section for study. Eight to twelve sessions, allowing at least two sessions for each chapter, may allow more adequate time for addressing all the principles.

Before the first session, you might ask participants to read at least the introduction. They might also read through the principles only and mark those they feel are most important to them or to your congregation. When the group gathers, list the principles that have caught the interest or concern of participants. Make it a point to read through and discuss these during your sessions together.

Leading a Session

Here is a suggested pattern for each of your study sessions.

Begin with prayer

Read

Read through the introduction or the principles that you have determined will be a part of your study during each session. You might read them aloud or ask those who may have read them ahead of time to summarize the principles and the background and applications. Note questions or comments that come from participants as you read.

Reflect

Ask participants to share what comes to mind from their own experience as you read together the principles. Encourage them to tell personal stories of how they have been involved or affected by the principles. For example, in connection with the preaching section, ask those who are willing to share their own experience of a sermon that had a particular impact on their lives. Or, in connection with the worship space section, you might invite participants to share descriptions of the church buildings in which they grew up. Help participants reflect on the principles in terms of their own faith life and practice.

Discuss

Move through the principles you have chosen for your session one at a time.

Read over each principle again and talk about it. Use questions that may come from the group or questions you have prepared ahead of time.

If you have assigned the principles to participants to research, ask those who may have done this work to share their discoveries or discussion questions.

Ask the pastor, musician, or a visiting resource person to comment.

Encourage participants to state the principle in their own words in order to be sure that all understand.

Take time to deal with questions or concerns that may remain for some people.

Evaluate

After your discussion of each principle, or toward the end of the session, be sure to think through the implications of the principles you have been discussing for the worship life of your congregation. For example, you might talk about what it would mean to consider modest changes in the layout of your worship space, or you might discuss the role that choirs play in your congregation's worship. Keep your discussion as practical as possible.

You might also encourage the group to evaluate the principles and to formulate a response, which, together with responses received from other congregations and individuals, will help the wider church continue the process of worship renewal.

Vision

You might end each session with a time for participants to project into the future what some of the enrichments of worship you have talked about might mean for the worship life of the congregation or their own worship life. Encourage them to be as specific as possible.

Close with prayer

RESPONSE FORM

Thank you for taking the time to study *Principles for Worship*. We invite you to join the dialogue and contribute your ideas to the ongoing renewal of worship.

Please send your response after you have studied the principles. When you refer to the document, use the numbering of paragraphs (for example, "Application M-15D") so it is clear to which specific points you are referring.

Send responses to Renewing Worship, Division for Congregational Ministries—Worship, Evangelical Lutheran Church in America, 8765 West Higgins Road, Chicago IL 60631. At www.renewingworship.org an electronic response form is available should you choose to respond in that way instead.

You may photocopy this form and use the spaces to write your comments. You may also send us a letter with your response. But please send a photocopy of pages 153-154 along with your letter so we can attach this important information to your comments.

1. What are the strengths of *Principles for Worship*? What about it or in it will be helpful to the church?

General

Language

Music

Preaching

Worship Space

2. In what ways has your study of the principles prompted growth in your understanding of worship? Which ideas in the principles reinforce, and which challenge, practices in your congregation?

General

Language

Music

Preaching

Worship Space

3. In what ways do you have difficulty understanding the principles? Are there areas in which they need further clarification?

General

Language

Music

Preaching

Worship Space

4. In what areas do you see weaknesses or find yourself disagreeing with the principles? How might they be improved or made more helpful to the church?

General

Language

Music

Preaching

Worship Space

5. Within the areas covered by these principles (language, music, preaching, worship space) what issues do you think are missing that may still need to be addressed?

Language

Music

Preaching

Worship Space

6. Are there other areas of worship not included in these four categories or in *The Use of the Means of Grace* for which study and guidance would be helpful?

INFORMATION ABOUT THIS RESPONSE

Please answer these questions and provide the requested information and include them with your response, whether it is filled in on this form or in a letter. If you are responding as an individual, please use section A. If you are submitting this response on behalf of a group, please use section B.

A   Individual Response

Name: _____

I am: _____ Female _____ Male

I am: _____ Lay
        _____ Lay-rostered
        _____ Congregational pastor
        _____ Pastor in specialized ministry/retired

I am: _____ Paid staff _____ Volunteer staff _____ Not staff

I am: _____ American Indian or Alaska Native
        _____ Black or African American
        _____ Hispanic or Latino/a
        _____ Native Hawaiian or other Pacific Islander
        _____ White
        _____ Other: _____

I am: _____ Under 25 _____ 25-50 _____ 50-65 _____ over 65

I have been a Lutheran (number of years) _____
Previous affiliation (or other affiliation, if not Lutheran) _____

Have you been part of a group that studied or discussed the principles? _____ Yes _____ No

B   Group response

ELCA Congregational ID # _____

If this response is not from an ELCA congregation or you do not know your congregation ID number, please note:

     Congregation: _____

     Location: _____

     Denomination: _____

Who prepared this response?

Is this _____ a personal report of a conversation _____ a formal response to which the group has agreed?

What is the nature of this group?

     _____ Congregation council or other congregational leadership group

     _____ Congregational study group made up primarily of lay people

     _____ Group of congregational pastors and/or other rostered leaders

     _____ Other: _____

How many hours were devoted to this study and discussion? _____ (approximate number)

Send completed responses to Renewing Worship, Division for Congregational Ministries—Worship, Evangelical Lutheran Church in America, 8765 West Higgins Road, Chicago IL 60631.

ISBN 0-8066-7003-7

9 780806 670034

90000